CONVERTED

CONVERTED

The Data-Driven Way to
Win Customers' Hearts

Neil Hoyne

PORTFOLIO | PENGUIN

Portfolio / Penguin
An imprint of Penguin Random House LLC
penguinrandomhouse.com

Copyright © 2022 by Neil Hoyne
Penguin supports copyright. Copyright fuels creativity, encourages diverse voices,
promotes free speech, and creates a vibrant culture. Thank you for buying an authorized
edition of this book and for complying with copyright laws by not reproducing, scanning,
or distributing any part of it in any form without permission. You are supporting writers
and allowing Penguin to continue to publish books for every reader.

Most Portfolio books are available at a discount when purchased in quantity for sales
promotions or corporate use. Special editions, which include personalized covers, excerpts,
and corporate imprints, can be created when purchased in large quantities. For more
information, please call (212) 572-2232 or e-mail specialmarkets@penguinrandomhouse.com.
Your local bookstore can also assist with discounted bulk purchases using the Penguin
Random House corporate Business-to-Business program. For assistance in locating
a participating retailer, e-mail B2B@penguinrandomhouse.com.

Library of Congress Cataloging-in-Publication Data
Names: Hoyne, Neil, author.
Title: Converted : the data-driven way to win customers' hearts / Neil Hoyne.
Description: New York : Portfolio/Penguin, [2022] | Includes bibliographical references and index.
Identifiers: LCCN 2021022910 (print) | LCCN 2021022911 (ebook) |
ISBN 9780593420652 (hardcover) | ISBN 9780593420669 (ebook)
Subjects: LCSH: Customer relations. | Internet marketing. | Marketing—Statistical methods.
Classification: LCC HF5415.5 .H69 2022 (print) | LCC HF5415.5 (ebook) |
DDC 658.8/12—dc23
LC record available at https://lccn.loc.gov/2021022910
LC ebook record available at https://lccn.loc.gov/2021022911

Printed in the United States of America
1st Printing

BOOK DESIGN BY CHRIS WELCH

To Liza, my love and partner on this incredible journey, and my children, Hamilton and Elizabeth, who provide the endless inspiration for it.

CONTENTS

INTRODUCTION

Digital marketing is about keeping the faith. The faith that you can seduce someone to buy more, vote differently, or just love your brand—all in a 250 x 250–pixel box as they're scrolling through websites, purposefully trying to avoid the message you're sending. It's about timing, extraordinary scale, and hoping that customers willing to pay full price don't find that 15 percent–off coupon code first. It's also a promise—help the customer reach their ambitions—while you get yours: their money.

My world, digital analytics, is the science behind proving that this faith hasn't been misplaced. That the messy pile of actions and metrics—the impressions, clicks, and conversions—wouldn't have happened without exposing users to that six-second pre-roll ad on their way to watching another unboxing video on YouTube. It's not a perfect world. Here's reality: shoddy, imperfect experiments that need ninety days but only get a dozen, and porous data sets that may represent as much of reality as a coin toss.

In this space, I've been an analyst, researcher, inventor, lecturer, programmer, and, most shamefully, the father of many forgettable slides of glossy funnels and Venn diagrams. A witness to and participant in billion-dollar successes and expensive failures driven by ego, ambition, and, much less often, pragmatism. A key player in the executive rallying cry to be more "data driven."

My latest gig, spanning more than a decade at Google, has given me the privilege to lead more than 2,500 engagements with our biggest advertisers. I have overseen initiatives that have acquired millions of customers, stretched conversion rates by more than 400 percent, and supposedly generated more than $2 billion in incremental revenue. (I don't know how the economists derived that number, but I like it, so I'm going with it. I have my sins too.) But, like for most analysts I know, it's the failures that made me second-guess my career choices, if not my sanity. It's a messy world, and I'm part of it. We all are.

The moments that make you think your finely tuned model might as well be a random number generator? I've had my share. I've seen researchers remove individual survey results—"outliers"—until the results matched the product manager's convictions. I've worked with executives who demanded absolute accountability for every dollar spent—until it came to buying the naming rights to a college football game. When their sales numbers showed they would have produced better returns had they wrapped their products in hundred-dollar bills and tossed them into the crowd, they questioned the data. And once, I had to partner with a particularly egregious group of consultants who pulled a revenue estimate right out of their asses. I know that because the footnote was literally "Replace these numbers I pulled out of my ass." They didn't even proof it. But nobody reads footnotes—apparently not even the board.

Well-intentioned executives and graduate students used to ask me about the secret to building a successful marketing organization. Was having one more success than your failures enough? Or was it found in embracing some Silicon Valley platitude like "Fail Faster"?

I wanted to know. And I have spent my career in search of an answer.

You'll find me in Google's Partner Plex, located on our Mountain View, California, campus, surrounded by relentlessly brilliant engineers who make serving up results to forty thousand search queries every second look effortless. While the engineers crank out code, manage systems, and do the heavy math, my team talks and strategizes with customers. We welcome them to our part of the campus with an AI-powered piano that composes its own music, a rainbow staircase of the latest search trends, and a virtual reality rig to paint in 3D. It's enough to make Willy Wonka wish he had a golden ticket.

We also have conference rooms. That's where the work gets done. They're more than your normal meeting space, because they're purpose-built for the tasks ahead. Stuffed with power and bandwidth, sugar and caffeine— courtesy of microkitchens tucked into a series of pull-out cabinets with "Drink" and "Eat" laser-etched into the sides. The conference tables, built from the same dark, laminated wood, could be branded with "Think." Here we collaborate with Google's largest customers on the future of their products and verticals.

Today I hold the title of Google's chief measurement strategist, but ever since starting out as an analyst, I was always curious to understand how executives made decisions based on the work my team produced, and why two companies often acted differently when shown the same data.

The question presented itself again and again. Why did companies use identical information to compete in entirely different ways? Over time, a pattern became clear. Most companies were focused on a single moment, a single sentence, a single interaction: Hey, take my offer! They were using the data to change creatives, colors, and targeting, changing words and tone across endless experiments. Anything to get the immediate *yes*—but everything was short term.

It made sense. CFOs demand accountability. Digital advertising gave it to them. They could instantly connect clicks to action. They spent a dollar and then the customer spent ten. It set the strategies and their weekly dashboards. But it was boxing the CMOs in. That one moment was all that mattered and all that was measured.

But to the CMOs, this made sense too. The larger they grew, the more data they collected, the better they could make the most out of each moment. Innovators, disruptors, or whatever new model the venture capitalists were funding would have to go through (and pay for) the same lessons themselves, setting fire to their balance sheets.

Until their competition sprinted ahead.

Some of these companies had come to the Partner Plex knowing they couldn't catch up by running the same race. They needed a new way to compete. We helped them find it. Instead of optimizing to the immediate, what if you built a business around long-term relationships with customers, using data to understand who the best customers were and what products they wanted to buy, then building around them? What if you could leave your competitors, with all of their data and their short-term thinking, just to poke around in the scraps?

The answer: You can. And it works incomprehensibly well.

The marketing success stories over the next decade will be about more than just clicks and conversions. They will be about people and conversations with customers that build into relationships.

A Digital Marketer Walks into a Bar . . .

. . . and asks the first person they see to marry them. Crazy, right? But that's what companies do. That's digital marketing. And if the marketing team asks enough strangers the question—maybe it's a hundred, maybe a thousand—eventually someone will say yes. The marketers give themselves one moment, one opportunity to drive a result, and they treat every interaction the same. They can change only so much—what they wear, which bar they walk into, maybe a word or two in what they say. And then the CEO asks: Why aren't more people saying yes?

Because others are playing a different game. They say hello, they start a conversation. They ask questions, actually *listen* to the answers, and let things develop. They begin to build a relationship, one step at a time, and then they ask themselves, "Is this going anywhere?" Their data tells them the answer—and they act on it.

This book is a field guide to this new terrain, an exploration loosely organized around three themes: conversations, relationships, and self-improvement. It's not meant to be read once, then left to sit on your shelf. I hope you'll turn to it often and share it with colleagues, excited by what you're learning. I want you to wear it out. (And then buy another copy, but that's just me.) It is a guide, filled with practical advice, but you won't find yourself lost in swamps of technical details. Along the way you'll see signposts to a website with additional content that supports the lessons in the book, a community of practitioners to engage with on your journey, and a developing set of tools designed to do much of the heavy lifting for you.

You can find the website at: http://convertedbook .com.

We'll start with conversations and the importance of interactions with customers: how to do it, what to expect, and also what not to do. The second section is all about relationships: your business depends on developing great ones while saving the time and money you'd spend on relationships that aren't going anywhere. The third, self-improvement, is all about looking inward— asking the right questions of yourself and avoiding the trap of self-delusion, which is sure to undermine any progress you make.

This adventure is yours. Ideas build on each other, so you can start at the beginning, indulging in everything offered. But each idea also stands on its own, so you can spend more time on the topics that speak to your own opportunities, curiosities, and closet fantasies and fit them to your purpose.

Everything you'll read here is inspired by real experiences, but not from one company or one industry. The lessons are in these experiences, not their particulars, so whether you are trying to sell products or solicit donations, it should all prove instructive.

Just remember: there are no certainties in marketing, as there are in the physical world. Days don't always follow nights. But while I can't tell you exactly how much your $10,000 will buy, I *can* give you the hard-earned lessons of how the greatest digital marketers use data to win the love of their customers, building unassailable relationships with almost mathematical precision. In this I have faith.

Welcome to church.

PART 1

CONVERSATIONS

1

LET'S TALK

It's a Saturday afternoon and a woman walks into a boutique shoe store, eyeing a pair of heels. Inevitably, she's approached by a salesperson. "Do you need any help?" The woman ignores the employee, lingers a moment longer on the high heels, and then exits the store.

Perhaps it's the style, the exorbitant price, or simply the inevitable pain of actually wearing them, but whatever her reason, she isn't interested in making the purchase. Or is she?

The woman returns later in the day and the same scene unfolds. The greeting, the fleeting interest, the quick exit. A third time, a fourth, a fifth, and then the next day, the same thing happens, and again the day after that. The staff keep adjusting their approach. A smile this time. A compliment the next. Anything to get her to buy the shoes she's been eyeing this whole time.

And then it happens. Nearly two weeks after her initial visit.

Those $450 worth of three-inch heels. Sold!

What happened differently this time? Most important, what lessons did the store take away to repeat this winning result? Not a thing. In reality, this woman never left home. Each of her—wait for it—262 visits occurred on the store's website. And nobody noticed. Nobody intervened. Nobody learned. Her experiences were lost in a spreadsheet filled with countless others—mothers, husbands, lifelong friends, and consummate professionals reduced to "conversions."

The store was able to track each of her visits. That was trivial. But they welcomed her with the same experience each time. Every visit was interpreted as interest, driving up their investment as they chased her with more online ads. Sure, they sold the shoes in the end. But even with their 40 percent margins, they ended up in the red.

And they never knew it.

The fact is digital marketers—myself included—are

Figure 1.1: The woman's purchase journey. Each block represents an actual interaction with the company's marketing efforts.

better at making statements than conversation. It's not hard to picture us at a bar, approaching strangers with the strongest possible thirty-second call to action and an almost painful sense of urgency. "You should marry me right now. Only one of me left!" God help you if you reply. We might even follow you around to other bars for the next two weeks. You know, just in case.

The first product sold through Google was a lobster. Someone sat at their computer in California, clicked on a search ad for a fresh Maine lobster, and bought a two-pounder. The next day, a live lobster was delivered in a box to their door, confused as hell about the past twenty-four hours.

It was a conversation that worked for *that* time.

But now that same person has dozens of devices and no shortage of options for their next purchase. Lobster-comparison sites. Lobster coupon codes. Lobster reviews. There are more than 4.8 million posts on Instagram hoping to inspire you with different ways to prepare your lobster. One lobster even became a social media influencer, which makes a telling statement about the influencer industry as a whole.

Today's conversations aren't so simple. They're bursting with nuance and opportunity. And most businesses haven't kept up, locked in the legacy that measuring the value of single interactions—"Marry me, now!"—must be more important than reaping the returns of a broader relationship over time.

Does it have to be this way? Absolutely not. We have conversations all the time in daily life. It's how human beings work. We read, we listen, we engage. Our ancestors were brought together by campfires, eliciting understanding, trust, and sympathy.* We have dinner with somebody, we get to know them; we spend time with family. We do it in business too; all the keynotes, Zoom video conferences, and trade shows with vendors handing out cheap plastic pens.

People think of brands and websites the same way. They talk about them almost as if they were people. I love this company! I hate *that* company. I love this website!

But does the company reciprocate that love? Probably not.

If any of this reminds you of your company's marketing, it's not your fault. I get it. Marketing has the decades-long pressure to prove its results, in order to justify its growth in good times and defend budgets in the bad.

---

* Polly W. Wiessner, "Embers of Society: Firelight Talk among the Ju/'hoansi Bushmen," *Proceedings of the National Academy of Sciences* 111, no. 39 (September 2014): 14027–35, DOI: 10.1073/pnas .1404212111.

And, in between, to fend off the misplaced belief that marketing is merely a cost center.

It only works until it doesn't. If customers see the same short messages and are pursued by the same relentless tracking everywhere they go, it's easier to be apathetic toward it all. But marketers are starting to see the value of conversation—not only because of the wealth of customer information it provides but also because it separates them from the competition. They stand out, and they triumph.

That makes a larger shift all but inevitable. Interactions between the best companies and their customers are changing from quick messages demanding an immediate response to deeper, more lasting conversations. "Buy now" behavior that would flop in a bar will get you left behind online too. You just won't survive as a marketing leader if you can't learn and respond to the signals customers are giving you.

At the end of the day, this is about looking at marketing through a different lens: the very human lens of conversation. We know how to do it already. We only need to learn how to do it in a different context.

2

STARTING SIMPLE

I sat at a noisy vegetarian bistro with a handful of retail marketing execs who had been trying to turn around their stale but promising brand. The CMO and his team had teased some rather lofty ambitions. They brought me in to offer feedback on their journey to a better place.

"We're excited about the opportunity here," they said. "We're going to digitally transform our business."

Usually, this is where I get concerned. *Digital transformation* is quickly earning its place in the upper echelons of bullshit business-speak, right next to *innovation*, *acceleration*, and *amplification*. Too often these kinds of grandiose ambitions end merely with a refreshed app icon and launching curbside pickup.

What this team unveiled was arguably worse: a $70 million software engagement to build out the most comprehensive data-management program the company had ever seen, uniting all their customer data, every touch point, everything imaginable.

It would be ready in only two and a half years.

I was appalled. *What's going on here?* These were skillful marketers, after all.

"Well!" they said. "It doesn't make a lot of sense to do anything until we get all of the data in place. Once we do, we'll be able to hire hundreds of data scientists to streamline all of our decision making."

They were really proud of this. Like it was a legitimate plan.

I couldn't help myself. "So you have a multimilliondollar project, you got the board to make this huge capital investment, you're not going to show any returns for three years—and you think this makes sense?"

"Well, yes, because the data has to be perfect first!"

I sat there thinking, *But what about your retail stores, which don't share any customer data back with you? Where is that coming from? Where does your brand value fit in? Or word of mouth? You'll still be missing large pieces of the conversation. What about the value of the data you have on customers today? Are you happy to give that opportunity up?*

The company's ambitions never played out. It took too long just to set up all the pieces. The board grew tired of waiting for results. The CMO is gone, and the brand shuffled between a few more private equity groups. But the legacy remains. Nobody will touch a similar project again.

Why You Need to Start Simple

When people feel they've lost control of circumstances, they tend to turn to high-involvement products that require hard work to fix things.* It's that January-gym-membership effect. Signing up feels like a tangible result, and that's what you're looking for. Does it work?

* Keisha M. Cutright and Adriana Samper, "Doing It the Hard Way: How Low Control Drives Preferences for High-Effort Products and Services," *Journal of Consumer Research* 41, no. 3 (October 2014): 730–45.

Not really. Eighty percent of those new customers won't make it past April.*

That's why the retailer was so proud of its software child. That's where most companies that are trying to tie together their data start. It's where they stop, too. Ask executives if their CRM system is helping business grow, and 90 percent will say no.†

Customer conversations are not about capturing every single interaction. That's exactly where most companies start with data, and it doesn't make sense.

Understanding your customers isn't about capturing every nuance of their behavior—every product they look at, and for how many milliseconds; how many times they place something in their shopping cart, then put it back on the shelf—without any sense of what actually matters. The fact is that the more information you try to gather, the more you miss, and the more you spend. Learn to recognize the signals that are important—and learn what not to obsess over. A marketer who can focus on what's necessary to move a business forward today is

---

* Rebecca Lake, "23 Gym Membership Statistics That Will Astound You," CreditDonkey, February 26, 2020, https://www.creditdonkey.com/gym-membership-statistics.html.

† Scott Edinger, "Why CRM Projects Fail and How to Make Them More Successful," *Harvard Business Review*, December 20, 2018.

ten times more valuable than one who gushes about the latest opportunity to connect everything in life to the internet. Come on. My flip-flops don't need to be connected to the internet, but I'm sure that someone somewhere is pitching that right now.

How to Start Simple

We have three principles to embrace. Nothing extravagant. This is about focus.

GET MOVING

The priority is simplicity. The more complicated the approach gets, the harder it is for us to make progress, the harder it is for us to have accurate data, and the harder it is for us to pull it. Keep things as simple and as lightweight as possible for now. Small teams. Swift action. Some of the most successful marketers I know spend no more than a couple hours setting up a database in the cloud and work from there; it'll be sloppy, and it might not scale well, but it's enough to get moving. Start with a workshop, not a factory. We don't need a huge CRM when a spreadsheet will do. We'll add more data as we go, but we'll do it with purpose. Every week I meet another company that's spent a year obsessing about how to store its data. The best marketers aren't doing that; they're obsessing over how they can *use* their data, keeping it simple, showing they can make money, and building from there.

START WITH PEOPLE

The finest source of truth is straightforward. It's money. If we made money from a customer, we know where that money came from, and we know who that customer is. That's the spreadsheet we're building. That's also the spreadsheet CFOs respect. They tend to care less about your leads or app downloads than about what's in the bank. Data organized on the basis of channels, campaigns, or products is the wrong way to look at this. Start with the people.

KNOW EVERYONE'S NAME

The third principle: we need to know as many names as possible, because that will help us tie everything together. Actual names. Email addresses. Loyalty program numbers. Something that allows us, when we look across systems, to know that the person over here is the same person there. The importance of this principle cannot be overstated. One entertainment company knows everyone by up to twenty-seven different IDs—one for each system, with no common connection. The company can't hold a decent conversation because they keep losing their place.

You need to be able to identify your customers. Offer incentives to encourage them to register for an account—exclusive content, promotional offers, coupon codes. (Just don't go overboard and give away your margin.) Use a single-sign-on provider like their Google or Facebook ID to ease the burden. Some companies get more creative with tools like email-campaign tagging to help identify customers across multiple devices.

The point is this: regardless of the approach you use, focus on identifying as many people as possible. Don't simply accept that only a few will give you their names before making a purchase. Work at it. Find the right balance, the approach that yields the most names at the lowest cost. It's that important.

Take What You Can Get

Don't wait to make use of the names you learn. Personalizing your marketing offers immediate benefits. Research found that adding the name of a recipient to the subject line of email marketing campaigns increased open rates by 20 percent and conversion rates by 31 percent while reducing unsubscribe rates by 17 percent. But bear this in mind: you've got to know just enough about your customers to get it right.*

* Navdeep S. Sahni, S. Christian Wheeler, and Pradeep K. Chintagunta, "Personalization in Email Marketing: The Role of Non-Informative Advertising Content" (Stanford University Graduate School of Business Research Paper No. 16-14, October 23, 2016).

You don't need ten thousand columns of data to have better conversations with your customers. It's not about recording everything. Start simple. Begin with data you're confident is accurate instead of trying to clean up everything that you've collected. Use names to keep things as consistent as you can. From there, you need to pay attention to what truly matters in your conversations. This is a skill that I'll teach you in the upcoming chapters.

There are companies that will sell you fully automated systems to conduct these conversations on your behalf. Some are better than others. But be careful. It's like asking your friend to talk to your crush at school. When your friend comes back and says, "They like you!" that's fantastic—but what do you really know about the exchange? Does your crush like you as a friend? As something more? Were they just being polite? It may lead to more questions than answers—and you'll still need to talk to your sweetheart eventually.

Be selective, don't overcomplicate . . . and then learn to listen.

3

ASK QUESTIONS

Travel is part of my gig. Even with the steroidal data and bandwidth on Google's campus, nothing can replace getting hands messy in the field, witnessing firsthand how store clerks and call center reps capture the interactions with customers, the silos that emerge when companies behave as two separate businesses—online and offline—united in brand name only, and all of the other idiosyncrasies that numbers still fail to represent. John le Carré had it right: "A desk is a dangerous place from which to watch the world."*

* John le Carré, *The Honourable Schoolboy* (New York: Penguin Books, 2011. First published 1977 by Alfred A. Knopf), 84.

Working in dozens of countries, you get attuned to the rituals of travel. The most fascinating come from the hospitality industry itself—a space where marketers are trying to capture data and understand and anticipate the needs of their guests, while still respecting their desire to book rooms with as little friction as possible. The proliferation of third-party agents like Expedia means that for most hotels, the conversation with customers doesn't begin until they arrive. You don't want a questionnaire when you check in after a long-haul flight. But what choices are hotels left with?

At the Ritz-Carlton, employees carry small notebooks they call preference pads in their uniform coat pockets. A decidedly low-tech method for capturing more customer data, but well named and highly functional. If the employee overhears a guest mention a personal preference— a type of music or beverage—it goes on the pad and from there to a single online profile, all in anticipation of future conversations.

But that's just the start. The real strength of the Ritz-Carlton and other top-performing hotels has been their extraordinary ability to direct those conversations in order to reap the information they need to benefit from them.

One such hotel has its own loyalty program but offers

guests benefits even if they indicate they've earned status in a competing plan. Why? Because that suggests a potentially valuable customer the hotel hasn't yet captured. It costs less money than you'd suspect, because perks like room upgrades are often space-available anyway. It's a small price to pay for learning a valuable signal that indicates a guest belongs to the lucrative business traveler segment and might be persuaded to switch allegiances.

Another hotel chain has fine-tuned every statement, every question its workers ask, into a precision experiment, testing different combinations of phrases across swaths of guests to see which provides the best insight into where they can improve as a company. Most hotel clerks will inquire, "So, how was your stay?" on checkout, which solicits nothing more than the all-but-requisite reply of "Fine." Instead, the clerks at this property ask, "Was there anything we could have done better?" because it's more likely to elicit an honest answer that's an opportunity to improve. The complaints they hear are stored with the customer's profile to make sure those things never happen again.

Some of the most successful marketing practices share this grounding in curiosity and inquisitive conversation. The marketers don't limit themselves to interpreting the data at hand. They see data as a window into a larger story, and they think about how they can be an active participant in the conversation. They respond to the customer with quick and nimble questions that tell them more about the customer's goals, advance the conversation, and deepen their understanding. That knowledge is power, and a significant advantage over competitors that lack the same.

How to Ask Questions

When I talk about asking questions, everyone immediately says, "Ah, we're going to send them an email survey! Again." Maybe. They have their place. But how many emails are your customers going to answer? Fewer than 3 percent.*

What's more, don't limit yourself to the big annual survey where you go out to all your customers with the same twenty questions in search of year-on-year metrics. Will answers next year help you? That's about measurement. This is about discovery and anticipation.

Don't limit yourself to the same old tools, and don't keep the power of questions to yourself. The curiosity

---

* "Email Trends and Benchmarks," Epsilon, Q2 2019.

must be shared. You want a lot of people in your organization asking questions all the time. It's about inspiring new ideas, satisfying curiosity, testing hypotheses, and making new discoveries. The key factor, as with capturing data, is to keep it simple and lightweight.

Here are three straightforward approaches to ask your customers more questions and engage them in deeper conversations.

The first is collecting more data from your website interactions. When people make a purchase, add one more question that can help you understand where things are headed next. Airlines that ask if a trip is for business or pleasure have a great insight into price sensitivity for upgrades.

Asking questions already? Mix them up. Rotate questions each week, gathering new insights that would have been missed if the same forms lingered unchanged for months or years. And don't obsess over asking 100 percent of people the same question. You'll find that the insights you glean are just as valid at about 5 percent.

Next is engaging people beyond your website. New tools let you survey your customers, or prospective customers, or even the competition's customers fast, easily, and cheaply. Google offers a product called Google Surveys that gives you access to an audience of several million people who are representative of the population and more than willing to answer questions about companies and products at a negligible cost. You can segment this audience too: by location, by a handful of demographics, even by people who have visited your website or shown interest in a competitor's product.

Finally, there's an emerging class of online chat products that enable you to engage directly with your customers in real time at given points in their journey, asking them questions or how you might help. These can be highly effective once set up, though they tend to consume more time and money than the alternatives.

I'm not arguing against your long-established methods here. My point is to encourage you to add more to your tool kit that makes it easier to ask more frequent and relevant questions of your customers.

Remember: discretion is required in asking anything of people. Here's a bad question for a first date: So, do you make a lot of money? There are better ways to get close to the answer. What do you do? Where do you live? So, iPhone or Android?*

---

* That may be the best question of all! One survey found that iPhone users make an average of $53,251 and Android users $37,040. Robert Williams, "Survey: iPhone Owners Spend More, Have Higher Incomes Than Android Users," Mobile Marketer, October 31, 2018.

Curiosity and practice will lead us to the right questions for your business. Want a little inspiration? Here are four ideas to get you started.

"ARE YOU BUYING THIS AS A GIFT?"

A staple of online shopping checkout pages everywhere, this question is often a last-ditch effort to upsell some deep-purple, faux-suede gift bag and a personalized note. And for most companies, that's exactly where it ends.

There's more to this question than an attempt to make a sale. As anyone who's choosing between jewelry from Tiffany and jewelry from Walmart knows, gift giving is a reflection of who you are. Research shows that when people buy gifts for others, it reinforces *their* connection with the brand. They spend more time shopping, comparing their options, so by the time they buy, they're committed. In one experiment, customers who bought gifts went on to spend 63 percent more with the brand in the next year.[*] Gift buyers had a 25 percent higher purchase frequency and spent 41 percent more on each shopping trip. The buyer's response to this question is a

[*] Andreas Eggert, Lena Steinhoff, and Carina Witte, "Gift Purchases as Catalysts for Strengthening Customer-Brand Relationships," *Journal of Marketing* 83, no. 5 (September 2019): 115–32.

signal that they could be worth more than a single purchase suggests.

"HOW MUCH DO YOU SPEND ON DINING OUT?"

Or on streaming movies, tax advice, or boutique hotels? Asking about spending—share of wallet, in industry-speak—yields an incredibly powerful response that can tell you if there's opportunity for growth. A research study of finance customers found that as they invested more, they diversified across more companies too.* Instead of putting $200,000 in one bank, they put $100,000 over here and $100,000 over there. If you've got two customers behaving the same way, you need to know if you've got 99 percent of their spending already, or just 10 percent—because that's the conversation with the bigger upside. They've got room to grow.

* Rex Yuxing Du, Wagner A. Kamakura, and Carl F. Mela, "Size and Share of Customer Wallet," *Journal of Marketing* 71, no. 2 (April 2007): 94–113.

"WHY DO YOU KEEP COMING BACK TO OUR WEBSITE?"

If someone keeps coming back to your website—five, ten, a hundred times—ask them why.

"When are you planning to buy a house?"

"What dates are you looking to travel?"

"Are you looking for anything in particular?"

Some customers, like our shoe buyer, may not be sure themselves, but at least you can segment those out from the ones who know, and act accordingly. Such questions can also reveal where the customer is in their journey, and when intervention on your part is required ("Do you plan to buy in the next three to six months?")— especially valuable for those big decisions that take some time to work through, like real estate, enterprise software, and automobiles.

"WHAT DO YOU LIKE MOST ABOUT US?"

Questions you ask can influence not just the answers you get but the customer's behavior too. Ask a neutral question ("How was your experience?") or a negative one

("Was there anything we could do better?") and you'll get more information; ask a positive question ("What do you like most about . . .") and you'll get more sales. In one test of retail customers, when the first question asked was positive, their spending went up 8 percent over the next twelve months.* The researchers also looked at B2B customers on a free trial. When a survey halfway through the trial led with "What do you like about your product experience so far?" they saw a 32 percent increase in sales of the paid product later on. Another study looked at financial services and found that positive questions led to more purchases and more engaged, more profitable relationships with customers—benefits that persisted even a year later.†

---

* Sterling A. Bone et al., "'Mere Measurement Plus': How Solicitation of Open-Ended Positive Feedback Influences Customer Purchase Behavior," *Journal of Marketing Research* 54, no. 1 (February 2017): 156–70.

† Utpal M. Dholakia and Vicki G. Morwitz, "The Scope and Persistence of Mere-Measurement Effects: Evidence from a Field Study of Customer Satisfaction Measurement," *Journal of Consumer Research* 29, no. 2 (September 2002): 159–67.

The Art of Asking Questions

What do we need to know about asking questions besides the questions themselves?

STRETCH YOUR VOCABULARY

How you phrase your questions will influence the answers you get; the way you order questions will make a difference too. The difference that words can make is significant. A case study featuring code.org found that changing a simple call to action—from "Learn More" to "Join Us"—helped improve the response rate by 29 percent.*

Harvard Business Review featured a study in which two groups of parents were asked what they felt was "the most important thing for children to learn to prepare them in life." One group was given a list of possible responses, and about 60 percent chose this one: "to think for themselves." The other group got the same question but in an open-ended format—and only about 5 percent

---

* *The Big Book of Experimentation*, Optimizely, 2017.

spontaneously came up with an answer along those lines.* Why? Well, without choices that narrowed their options, *they* were forced to think for themselves. Was giving their children the ability to think for themselves really what parents valued, or was it simply the obvious choice in a list they were given?

You need to experiment. Try different questions, ask the same questions in different ways, and ask at different times. Watch how customers respond and adjust, just as you would in any other conversation.

RESTRAIN YOURSELF

I worked with a real estate company that began every conversation with interested customers with seventy-three questions. When are you thinking about buying your house? What type of house is it? Is this your first or second house? Will you live there, or is this an investment property? How long do you think you're going to keep the house? Do you plan on renovating the house?

The reality: in order to score them as a potential buyer,

* Alison Wood Brooks and Leslie K. John, "The Surprising Power of Questions," *Harvard Business Review,* May–June 2018.

all they really needed was a credit rating and a price range. But they were trying to figure out who would actually end up buying a home three to six months out.

None of their questions gave them the signal they were looking for. But they annoyed a lot of people. A lot of applicants dropped out around question 20. It was too complicated; they left. Asking too many questions is a two-time loser: you'll bury yourself in data and you'll turn off potential customers. Less is more.

DON'T JUST SIT THERE

The best question in the world is a poor question if you don't have any way to apply the answer.

Hey, do you like to go snowboarding?

Yeah! Is there any snow?

Nope.

Then why did you ask me that question?

Just curious.

Before you ask a question, ask yourself how you'll respond based on the answer. Don't ask somebody how much they're spending if it's not going to change what you do next. Collect with intention.

AND DON'T GET COMPLACENT

People are who they are, but at the same time, circumstances change frequently. Use the data you gather right away, and recognize that anything you learn has a limited life span. You'll have to ask the same customers the same questions again later, because their answers will change. There's no standard for how quickly, so asking customers routinely is a good practice. When their answers suggest behavior is changing, a more comprehensive study may be needed to understand why.

*D*on't make the mistake of assuming that you can learn everything you need to know about a customer just by collecting data and watching them. That's not conversation; it's eavesdropping. And it's creepy.

So ask questions, but do it with purpose. You're in a conversation with your customers, whether you know it or not. Join it.

4

EMBRACE HUMAN NATURE

One thing that data-driven companies try to do is insist that human beings are perfectly rational, that they make decisions purely based on price and value and features. They want the fastest website and the quickest shipping times; the data explains everything.

But we've actually found a lot of opportunity in looking beyond the data to recognize the reality of human behavior: it's often irrational.

A growing B2B distributor was struggling with its online experience. As the company acquired partners and competitors, each brought their own proprietary tools for managing inventory. Searching for anything—product availability, pricing, or shipping times—meant pulling data from dozens of systems held together by a patchwork of code. Customers were waiting up to thirty seconds for their results. Long-held beliefs said that speed was everything, and the data supported this. One study found that a one-hundred-millisecond delay could lead to a 7 percent decrease in conversion rates.*

Worried that customers were more likely to leave than suffer through the delays, the company invested millions in infrastructure and consultants—and finally connected the systems into a single, state-of-the-art cloud platform that delivered the same results in a fraction of the time. This seemed like the smart thing to do.

But this company's payoff? Sales didn't grow. Complaints did. Customers felt products were missing, and satisfaction scores dropped. When asked, more than 70 percent of visitors preferred the *old* platform. What happened?

We're only human. People want to see signals that other people are doing work on their behalf. Researchers found these signals in the kitchen, where they learned

---

* "Akamai Online Retail Performance Report: Milliseconds Are Critical," Akamai.com, April 19, 2017.

that when cooks and cafeteria diners could see each other, customers' satisfaction with their meal went up 17 percent.*

It turns out this expectation extends to digital interactions as well. A follow-up study found that although many websites try to deliver objectively faster performance, their customers may judge the service less valuable if they can't "see" the labor involved.† That's especially so for search results. A status bar scrolling across the screen improves the perceived value of the results even if they take longer to deliver. The results feel more trustworthy and more satisfying. People are willing to wait as long as sixty seconds over instantaneous delivery—just so long as the delay offers insight into the work that's allegedly being done.

Sure enough, when the B2B site added a loading message and a delay of a few seconds to make it seem credible, customer feedback improved.

---

* HBR Editors, "Cooks Make Tastier Food When They Can See Their Customers," *Harvard Business Review*, November 2014.

† Ryan W. Buell and Michael I. Norton, "The Labor Illusion: How Operational Transparency Increases Perceived Value," *Management Science* 57, no. 9 (September 2011): 1564–79.

Why You Need to Embrace Human Nature

We all have that one friend who ticks all the boxes but still can't get a date. They have the job, the looks, and the money. The math is on their side, but somehow it all adds up to nothing more than another weekend alone.

Marketing, like dating, isn't an objective affair.

Marketers often assume their customers are logical, rational beings who weigh the pros and cons in each choice they face—so surely they'll value the website loaded with the most products and blessed with the fastest load time. This assumption is true to a degree; data clearly supports the case that people abandon extremely slow sites. But there's nuance in how people behave, and sometimes what they do isn't what anyone might initially expect. That's what makes us human. There's a huge opportunity awaiting marketers who understand this reality—and act on it in how they present themselves or frame choices to their customers.

How to Make Human Nature Work for You

Increasingly, marketers are incorporating behavioral science into their marketing plans. And you don't have to learn everything about the discipline to reap the benefits. What I'm about to tell you is just enough to guide you through the implementation of these practices: where to consider other factors or tweak the approach, based on your circumstances. Ready for a peek behind the curtain? Here are some behavioral science techniques to get you started.

TEASE THE FINISH LINE

Whether it's setting up a new account or earning loyalty status, nobody likes to start from the beginning. It's an uphill battle and they're staring up from the base of the mountain. Instead, give them the sense that they've made progress already and the wind is at their back. A process may have eight steps, but you'll see better completion rates if you present it as a ten-step process where the user has already completed the first two steps. If you're trying to get the customer to take more steps in the future, present it as a missing piece in their journey. ("Your account is 90 percent set up!")

The initial title of an advertisement encouraged users to enter their business information into a new product, Google My Business, with a straightforward prompt:

Own a business?
Add it to Google Search now to make sure people find you

NO THANKS   YES, START NOW

Figure 4.1

Together, the title and button emphasized the start of the process. In a test case, Google marketers supplied the prompt below to a separate group of users, placing them just shy of the finish line. In reality, both groups were starting from the same place.

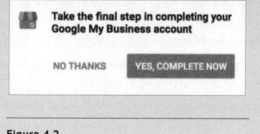

Figure 4.2

The result: the test version saw customer-acquisition rates increase by 20 percent, saving the equivalent of nearly $2 million in advertising.

STRESS THE SCARCITY

When something is in short supply, we perceive it as more valuable. That's the power of scarcity.* And people perceive a loss to be twice as powerful as a gain of the same size. That's loss aversion.†

Scarcity manifests itself in everything from limited-time offers to products with only a few left in your size. Urgency: *One room left.* Warning: *15 people looking right now!* (Some travel sites have been accused of displaying random numbers,‡ but in my experience, many are accurate. What they don't share is that the fifteen people are often looking at different days.)

Loss aversion lies behind marketing pitches such as product discounts, those same warnings on limited

* Robert D. Cialdini, *Influence: The Psychology of Persuasion*, rev. ed. (New York: Harper Business, 2006).

† Amos Tversky and Daniel Kahneman, "Advances in Prospect Theory: Cumulative Representation of Uncertainty," *Journal of Risk and Uncertainty* 5 (1992): 297–323.

‡ Ophir Harpaz (@OphirHarpaz), "Ok this is really funny, check this out. I was in the process of booking a flight via @OneTravel. Trying to make me book ASAP, they claimed," Twitter, October 16, 2019, https://mobile.twitter.com/ophirharpaz/status/1184486445039 411201. He checked the underlying code on a travel website and found the number was randomly generated.

inventory, and promotional bonuses. All are powerful messages to drive someone to act now or miss out later.

In another Google experiment, adding a simple headline of "Don't miss out on expert help" increased the program's click-through rate by 53 percent.

> ℹ️ **Don't miss out on expert help**
> Have an AdWords Account Specialist review your campaigns, for free. Reserve your spot today.
>
> Learn more | Dismiss

Figure 4.3

GATHER THE CROWD

Peer pressure—it's not just for middle school. When people aren't sure how to behave, they look to the behavior of others as a guide.* This is why 82 percent of Americans have said that they seek recommendations from friends and family before making a purchase.[†] In marketing, this can mean celebrity endorsements or mentioning how many customers have taken a particular action, such as jumping in line on a wait list or buying the latest sunglasses. It even works with product ratings. So when you're looking at that rocket-powered hang glider, remember that conversion rates jump 270 percent for products with at least five reviews compared with those that had none. (But buy that hang glider anyway. Because it's awesome.)

* Cialdini, *Influence*.
† Todd Patton, "How Are Consumers Influenced by Referral Marketing?" getambassador.com, 2016.

In a Google experiment, users who were shown a booking table with some time slots grayed out, indicating that others were scheduling times too, had an 87 percent higher click-through rate.

Get free advice from our AdWords Experts.

Get off to the right start. Talk with an AdWords Expert to finish setting up your account.

Click one of the time slots below to set a calendar reminder to call an AdWords Expert. Times in blue are still available.

Wednesday, December 03	Thursday, December 04	Friday, December 05
9:00am	10:30am	9:30am
11:30am	12:00pm	11:00am
2:30pm	3:20pm	3:30pm
4:30pm	4:00pm	4:30pm

Figure 4.4

PLANT A SEED

When you expose someone to stimulus—such as a word, image, or statistic—it changes how they respond to future interactions. That's priming. Most marketers fixate on the lighter side of the space: colors that convey emotion or imagery that reinforces a particular attribution, like clouds to softness. There can be a darker side to it too. One study found that when Asian American women were primed with a question about their racial identity, they achieved higher scores on a math exam.* When they were primed with a question about their gender, the opposite was true. Priming is a useful technique, but the dark side of this force is strong. Guide, don't manipulate. Lean into your Jedi training, and you'll be fine.

* Margaret Shih, Todd L. Pittinsky, and Nalini Ambady, "Stereotype Susceptibility: Identity Salience and Shifts in Quantitative Performance," *Psychological Science* 10, no. 1 (January 1999): 80–83.

The original title ("Built for gamers") on a pop-up ad for YouTube Gaming did nothing to prime the people who saw it:

Built for gamers
YouTube Gaming: all gaming, 24/7
GO TO GAMING

Figure 4.5

But the test variation did:

Are you a gamer?
Join other gamers on YouTube Gaming
JOIN GAMERS NOW

Figure 4.6

By priming the audience ("Are you a gamer?") and then inviting them to join their peers ("JOIN GAMERS NOW"), the YouTube team saw a 2.3-time increase in the number of users who clicked on the message.

We are what we are: humans. *Emotional, lovable bundles of behavior that don't always make sense. Understanding the nuances of human behavior allows you to have better conversations with your customers. That's behavioral science, and no, you don't need a doctorate in the field to put it to work for you; learn the basics—and go get something done. Embracing irrationality in how you interact with customers will serve you better than presenting a rational argument alone.*

5

TAKE A HINT

In real life, understanding the full story of a conversation can be a lot harder than just listening to the words. That's because the words someone uses don't always tell you what they're really trying to say. When you ask your frowning partner how they're feeling and they say, "Fine," are they *really* fine? When you ask a parent what they want for their birthday and they shrug and say, "I don't need anything," are they really asking you to surprise them with something special?

Some companies have a harder time reading hints than others. I worked with an automaker that suffered from that problem. They were investing millions of dollars into a marketing mystery where manufacturers, regional management, and individual dealers were promoting the same vehicles, all with the coordination of a first-time figure skater. Separate budgets. Separate tactics. Separate websites. The automaker knew that cars were selling—they were building them, after all—but the conversations that made the deals happen were unintelligible.

This carmaker's challenge was born from a well-intentioned pursuit of building a customer funnel. It's the marketing equivalent of saying, "This is how I want a date to go: I'm going to pick her up and take her to a restaurant, and then I'm going to compliment her on her outfit, and then I'm going to pay for dinner, and she's going to think I'm a better person, and then we're going to go out again. (Maybe next time we'll kiss.)" Is that how it actually goes? Not really. Human interactions aren't always linear.

But this hasn't stopped teams from sitting around a table and proclaiming the opposite. A pharmaceutical company may draw a straight line from a visitor recognizing their symptoms to that visitor talking to their doctor and decide that's the ideal path. A retailer might decide that getting visitors to add things to their shopping cart is the key step in moving from consideration to purchase. Once the steps are codified, campaigns are designed to optimize for them, and that only reinforces the team's belief that that's how consumers behave. It's not a funnel as much as a self-fulfilling prophecy.

For this automaker, the vehicle customizer tool stood in for the checkout process. The higher the price of the model the customer chose, the more recognition the marketing team bestowed on the advertising channel that brought the customer there. The manufacturer did its job; it built the funnel and did its best to guide visitors from top to bottom. The rest was in the hands of the dealer, whom it conveniently recommended as a closing note.

The numbers moved, but never in sync with the expectations. Excuses flowed. *Dealers dropped the ball. Customers bought; we just never heard about it. Online drove just a small slice of sales, and we couldn't rise above the noise.* Marketing optimization became a practiced ritual in faith more than data.

But that data was there all along, whispering heretical thoughts. The carmaker's solution started with recognizing the need to challenge its own prophecy.

They replaced their assumptions with testing—and found no correlation between the car customizer and making a purchase. It was entirely random. The high-end customizers that they thought were überprofitable? Experimentation and survey data suggested that those customizers were just teenagers out to build dream cars and enthusiasts expressing their aspirations, not buyers with any real intentions of purchasing. The marketers were spending millions in advertising dollars to reach people whose signal said, "I can't even afford the base model—so I might as well put these $20,000 rims on it. Oh—and the leather-trimmed door sills too!" And those people weren't even buying cars.

The marketers had locked on to the wrong hint. They had talked themselves into the belief that their customers wanted to have a conversation they imagined from their desk.

What *was* the right hint? After a fair amount of effort, they found that looking for financing information was a much more reliable signal of intent. Almost no one went to that corner of the website—because nobody searched for APRs or leasing terms unless they were close to a purchase. That's the conversation the carmaker's best prospects wanted to have. Once the marketing team locked on *that* hint, the numbers began moving in a way that made sense.

Why Hints Matter

Questions aren't enough. People may not know the answer or care to give an honest one. If you ask people how they heard of your business, some are certain to mention advertising channels you don't use. We even ran a diagnostic survey one time asking: "What color is the red ball?" One in five people said orange. Sigh. But you can still look at combinations of other hints—where small things come together in surprising ways—and carry the conversation forward.

Take product returns, which have retailers eating more than $640 billion in losses each year.* So what do you do? You could *ask* customers if they're going to return their purchase, but it's hard to imagine anyone admitting to that degree of pessimism. However, there may be a few telltale hints lurking beneath the surface. The order history of the habitual returner. The same product ordered in a scattering of sizes. One study found that when shoppers interact with products, zooming in to see the texture of the fabric or rotating it to see its

---

* IHL Group, "Retailers and the Ghost Economy: $1.75 Trillion Reasons to Be Afraid" (research report, 2015).

appearance from multiple sides, they're less likely to return their purchase later on.* The hypothesis: shoppers who use those functions are better informed about the product they're buying.

Google faces the same challenge in B2B settings. One of Google Cloud's big products is Google Workspace, a collaboration package that includes corporate versions of software such as Gmail. Paid advertising drives most of the new users, but with its thirty-day free trial, marketers could be sitting for up to four weeks before they can tell if a conversation is working.

The marketers could ask people how serious they are about buying. (But they haven't tried the product yet.)

They could ask about the size of their organization. (The answer hasn't revealed much in the past.)

And they can't just keep asking them questions without turning the conversation into an interrogation. Who wants that? (Frustration with the registration form, and they bail.)

* Prabuddha De, Yu (Jeffrey) Hu, and Mohammad Saifur Rahman, "Product-Oriented Web Technologies and Product Returns: An Exploratory Study," *Information Systems Research* 24, no. 2 (December 2013): 998–1010.

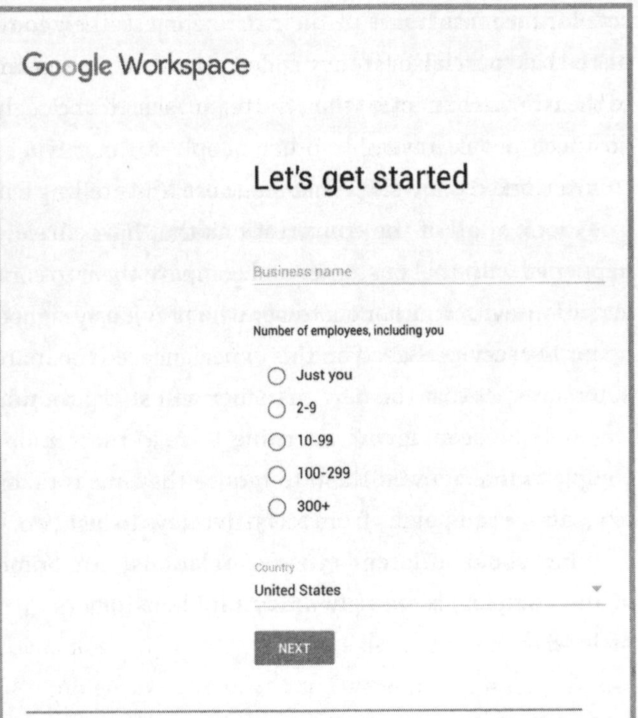

Figure 5.1: The Google Workspace registration form

Instead, the marketers analyze what's happened in the conversation so far. The number of times someone visited the Google Workspace website. The pages on the site that they read—and for how long. If they came during regular business hours in their time zone. If they completed the tutorial, or if they added others on their team to the trial account. And then the team asks: How closely do these people resemble other people we met where things worked out well? What are these hints telling us? They look at all of the conversations that have already happened with that customer and compare them to conversations with another customer who previously signed up for the service. Based on this experience, do the marketers predict that the new customer will stick around? Or never be seen again? Learning to read those more complex hints allowed them to reduce the time it takes to optimize campaigns from forty-five days to just two.

What about different types of relationships? Some of the complex, seemingly crazy hints customers give include:

- People who add apologetic messages when purchasing gifts are the least concerned about price. They're trying to right a wrong and are more likely to respond to upsells such as faster deliveries or larger arrangements. Cost is the furthest thing from their mind.

- For some credit cards, people who wait seven to ten days to bite after a promotional offer are more likely to keep the service after the first year. The best explanation is that these customers are intrigued by the promotion, such as free frequent-flier miles, but that's not their only motivation. Those who sign up right away may be leaping at an offer that's too good to refuse or surprised they were even offered credit in the first place. They are more likely to be gone several months later.

- When shoppers add an item to their cart, it's seen as a big step forward. They are a click away from buying. Let loose the stalking ads! It can work. But the act of curation—modifying items in the cart—is a consistently stronger signal that someone is closing in on the purchase.

What does it all mean? This type of acumen is essential in understanding how a conversation is progressing before it reaches its conclusion, when the customer decides to purchase or leave forever. It's also essential to understand that the signals customers are sending may not be the ones you're looking for. But the signals are still out there for your business. You just need to look for the right ones. Let's talk about how to do it.

How to Read Hints

START WITH THE PROBLEM

Don't start with the need to use the software. Please. Start by thinking about the question you need to answer: What is the likelihood this customer will do *this* in the next thirty days? Subscribe to a service? Ask for help? Upgrade their features? Be profitable? (Or not.) You get the idea. And make sure your business will adjust course, if needed, once you know the answer.

CHOOSE YOUR WEAPON

Some marketers will use a spreadsheet to look at simple correlations. A conversation (or transaction) in every row. In column one: How much was it worth to the company? In column two: Did they order through the mobile app? Column three: Did they use this particular feature on our website? They'll add the numbers up, sort the results, and say that people who ordered here and used this feature returned the product less often.

But for everything else, we're going to need something more powerful. Some way to filter through not only hundreds but thousands, maybe even millions, of different signals working in combination to understand which signals matter—and which ones are just noise.

Machine learning can do this work for us.

Yes, I said it: machine learning. Don't be scared. You got this.

I recognize that machine learning can be a complicated, technically dense, PhD-level subject. You don't have to turn it into that type of expedition. The iPhone in your pocket has roughly ten thousand times more processing power than the Apollo computer that put humankind on the moon, but that doesn't mean you have to use it to build a rocket of your own. (Unless you're Elon Musk.) While machine learning programmed by master practitioners can guide a self-driving car or beat the best of us at our own games, you can also use it simply to replace some of the tedious work you might otherwise do by hand.

Your customer may have done a thousand different things on your website. We're just combining your data and a lot of computing power so we can ask, "Hey, smart computer science data thing! Can you tell me if any of these actions matter?"

But how does this work, exactly? Practically speaking, you provide the source data ("Here are all the things we observed about our customers") and the results (such as revenue, lifetime value, satisfaction score). Machine learning then tries to figure out the combination of customer characteristics that can either predict the outcome of each conversation or optimize for the best results.

MIND YOUR DATA

You might be surprised to learn where as much as 80 percent of our time went in many machine learning projects: cleaning up the data. It can be an absolute, demoralizing mess. You find records shipping products to locations that don't exist, others selling products in stores that weren't open, and duplicate customers who created new email addresses simply to qualify for discount coupons.

It's getting easier, but it's still a crucible that marks every machine learning project. Take it one step at a time. When you move into the next step below, build from the data you know is already in good shape, like your transaction or web analytics data, and see if it uncovers anything useful. Then clean and expand for deeper insights.

SET A TARGET

Over the next 180 days, rally the resources needed to work toward answering the question that you set for your business at the outset. What are the hints that might tell you the answer? It's an approachable challenge. It's got a target, and it will force decisions and compromise. You need to go end to end, identifying a business problem, thinking through the question you need to ask, and learning how to pull and clean the data that's necessary to answer it.

The record for a company I've worked with stands at four days—and it's not only because of their data scientists. What you'll find when you run such a test isn't that the machine learning is burdensome. It's not a lack of talent and data that will hold you back. The real challenges lie in your internal processes: working collaboratively to define the problem, cleaning the data, passing approvals, implementing the solution live for customers. Jump in, try it, and learn. Once you get through the first round, identify the bottlenecks and run it again.

Tips for Picking Up What Your Customers Put Down

Marketers are quick to hand off a technical project like machine learning to somebody "who does machine learning" and let them run with it. Don't. You have a role to play in deciding where it's most important to read the hints and how you bring what you learn into the conversation. Here are some starting points.

MEASURE, ALWAYS

This one is pretty straightforward: you need to measure your outcome, consistently. If you're trying to predict how often somebody will talk about you (word of mouth) or how they feel about your brand, you need a reliable way to measure the result. Otherwise there is no way to understand the accuracy of your prediction—and no way to know whether what you're anticipating will actually come true!

EXPLORE THE WORLD

If you've only tried meeting people at the altar, you won't know much about the dating scene, because you've only been to one place and looked for one type of person. There's nothing new that machine learning can tell you about your customers unless you take the plunge and explore what the world has to offer—asking different types of questions, challenging your assumptions, and seeing what the answers suggest. Go out and have a look, say hello to different types of people. It's a different way of thinking about bias, beyond the usual concern of avoiding leading questions that influence your results.

Bias can also lie in the limits of the data you've gathered. We can build predictions only based on the types of conversations we've had in the past. The limited ways in which you've tried to reach people, and the focus on reaching only certain types of people, may bound your ability to predict beyond them. I point this out not only to convey the limits of what you can do in this space but also to encourage you to always explore new areas, capture that data, and understand how conversations go when you try something different.

DON'T REINVENT WHEELS

Some aspects of consumer behavior are predictable. In a few chapters, we'll introduce one statistical model for understanding the value of not just conversations but entire relationships. Just know that these types of models might work better than machine learning, and they're already built. They require less of your own data. Take the shortest route to the answer that you can and move on.

You'd be surprised how many companies turn to machine learning for the wrong reason. They'll say: I'm going to build the model myself, because I'm different, and my conversations are special. Please. Don't get carried away with yourself. Understand that sometimes these established models outperform machine learning programs built from scratch. Accepting that reality can save you a lot of time and frustration.

As a marketer, it's not your job to know how all of the models and techniques work, but it is your responsibility to know what might be out there and to connect the dots for your analysts. That means finding the middle ground. Pay attention to the emerging ideas in this space from academics who haven't yet commercialized their work: in journals, at conferences, in research papers. Read the abstracts at the beginning and check out the managerial implications at the end. Broaden your mind. Let your data scientists and analysts sort through the middle. For everything else, machine learning will probably save you some time. Choose wisely.

REMEMBER: THINGS CHANGE

The auto manufacturer who opened this chapter shifted the focus of its messaging. Now everything was all about nudging the conversation toward how the customer would pay for their new car. Vehicle sales improved and felt pretty measurable. Everything was going great—until it wasn't.

As soon as I went to the manufacturer's website, I could see why: finance offers *everywhere*. Dazzling photos of cars replaced with financing offers. Dealership locators–turned–lease calculators. Calls to action, email campaigns, social media posts—all promoting ways to afford your next vehicle.

Too much. Time to rerun the model with updated data. Time for something fresh.

Marketers are always looking to optimize. Once interest in financing became the measure of their success, it took precedence over all other content—even if opulent interior pictures, detailed spec sheets, and dealer locators were also necessary to get the buyer to the point of purchase.

It's like wearing an outfit one day that everyone loves. Wear it the next day, and the day after, and for the next few weeks, and the response will change. Tastes change too. Markets and competitors change.

Insights are not eternal truths. Don't ever stop asking questions, running tests, looking for signals. Use what you can for today, but invest in finding answers for tomorrow.

*A*t any time, you're in the middle of hundreds of conversations with countless, sometimes conflicting hints. Success is understanding which ones you should pay attention to, anticipating the needs of your customers, and acting accordingly. Machine learning will help you make sense of it all. Start with the opportunity for your business, keep your actions nimble, and be mindful of how everything you've done in the past will shape how you can respond in the future. Then have at it.

6

GUIDE THE CONVERSATION

I f you couldn't tell, I'm a very important person—a VIP. An exalted shopper. Worthy of free priority shipping, first access to sales, and exclusive coupons.

At least, that's what the retailer's email told me.

I had to gloat to my wife, who, despite purchasing nearly three dozen times from that same retailer in the past year, was still expected to pay full price. I bought socks. Possibly a shirt.

Maybe my purchases were high margin?

Maybe men's fashion was their focus?

Maybe I'm just more likable? I did use more emojis with their customer service. ☺

A friend at the retailer set me straight: I was costing them too much money. I wasn't a great customer. I was a bad one.

When leading companies measure customer conversations, they also measure cost. How much does each interaction with a customer cost the business, and what is the total cost of the conversation? Some companies measure every minute they spend on the phone with you, multiply it by the cost of the customer rep's time, and keep a running total to determine if you're worth the effort.

This retailer was doing the same thing, but they were focused on the advertising cost of the conversation. They were counting my clicks. My indecision, my insistence on price shopping or waiting for the right sale, meant that I had clicked on more ads than their average customer. I was squeezing their bottom line.

The marketing team had a choice to make. They could stop showing me ads, cut their costs, and hope I'd come back on my own. But that risked losing me to a competitor. And while I was cutting into their margins, I was still profitable. Their response was to get involved in the conversation, guiding my behavior.

Their program invited me and other high-cost customers to share in special benefits that we could access only by going to an exclusive site built just for us. Click on their advertising, come to them through their regular website, and they'd treat me like my wife: nothing special. (Only in this context, I hasten to add.) Go directly to their special site—costing them nothing—and I'm a VIP. Now I knew their secret. And I still felt pretty special.

Why You Need to Guide the Conversation

It's not enough to listen and anticipate. We need to say something back, to influence where the conversation goes.

But most marketers have only two things to say.

"Here's the exact same thing I said the first time! Would you buy it already?"

Or . . .

"Okay, but I'm just going to follow you around the internet until you say yes."

The sooner we join the conversation, and the better our reply, the more likely we are to shape it to our liking.

It's not just about controlling costs, either. It certainly can be, but it's also about telling the company's story, building trust, and increasing sales too.

What the retailer was saying to me with its VIP program was "Hey, I'm cool if we hang out. I just don't want to go out to another three-star restaurant. How about a beer and a sandwich?" They just used different words.

How to Guide the Conversation

I can't tell you what to say in every circumstance. Not unless you want me whispering through a little microphone in your ear. (You shouldn't want that. I share too many details and talk way too fast.) What I can do is give you some examples, starting simple and growing in complexity, to inspire your thinking.

KEEP THINGS FRESH

This is something only a handful of websites actually do. For the rest, whether you visit one time or a hundred times, it's the same message, the same content, the same experience. The most you'll see is a small recommendation engine: *You looked at this on your last visit; go see it again!* Or maybe a personal greeting: *Welcome back, Neil!* And that's where it ends.

But in a conversation, we need to customize the user's experience. If it's their first visit to our site, maybe we don't want to push on them to buy now; maybe instead we say, *Hey, let's introduce you to our products. Let's educate you about their value.* If it's their tenth visit, maybe now the message is a nudge toward buying.

The variations are endless. The basic idea is to start changing what you say based on how many times you've met.

SAVE YOUR BREATH

Remember our shoe shopper, who visited a website 261 times before finally buying a $450 pair of shoes on visit 262? We found in an internal study that only 2 to 3 percent of online shoppers are that egregious—thank goodness—but they can absorb as much as 10 percent of your advertising budget. These shoppers, even if they buy something, end up costing you money.

Find the customers who are costing too much time or too many resources or are returning too many purchases. Then find a way to spend a bit less on them so you can spend more elsewhere. Most advertising platforms allow you to exclude them from future marketing campaigns or after certain points in the conversation, and experiment to see if they come back and purchase on their own.

DON'T WALK AWAY EARLY

We talked earlier about using data to anticipate what's coming next in a conversation.

In one project, a hotel company found guests were returning to the website a few days before a reservation, often through paid search advertising. But instead of booking again, they were confirming the details of their upcoming stay. One hundred forty thousand dollars in advertising wasted each year without any new bookings.

Their solution: Seventy-two hours before the beginning of a reservation, start sending emails with all the information the guest needed for their trip. The location. The directions from the airport. The phone numbers, in case they needed help. A big banner on the top: "Everything is confirmed. No need to do anything else." Absolutely gorgeous.

The emails were free. And the company went on to lose even more money.

Wait. What?

It turns out that sending these emails not only kept people from needing to confirm the details of their stay but also reminded some forgetful business travelers that they were about to be charged for a room they'd forgotten about as part of a trip they thought they had long ago canceled. The company saved $0.05 for an ad click and lost a $200 booking.

In the next round through, the company learned how to predict who might cancel and excluded them from the reminders altogether. That's the cadence. You listen. You ask. You learn. Or you do nothing and just suffer the loss.

We never know how customer conversations will turn out. That's what makes them fun. But we have a part to play. We can choose what to say next. We can cut our costs. We can influence the result. It's time to be more than a passive observer. And we have to recognize that all customers are not created equal, and act on that too. That's where we're headed next.

PART 2

RELATIONSHIPS

7

LET'S TALK ABOUT YOUR FRIENDS

I get the same questions every time I tell the story of the shoe woman who clicked on so many ads before buying that the retailer took a loss on the sale.

What if she came back?

What if she just needed time to get to know us?

What if now she's fallen for our brand, decided we were destined for each other?

I get it. Acquiring a new customer is anywhere from five to twenty-five times more expensive than retaining an existing one.*

---

* Amy Gallo, "The Value of Keeping the Right Customers," *Harvard Business Review*, October 29, 2014, https://hbr.org/2014/10/the-value-of-keeping-the-right-customers.

But did she come back?

No. She didn't. Never again.

Here's our ultimate objective: don't treat every customer as a one-and-done, and at the same time, don't let the difficulty of meeting new customers scare us into desperation with anyone who shows the slightest bit of interest. It starts with that first conversation, but what should you do next?

Let's say we weren't talking about just one indecisive person and their footwear. Let's say you met a hundred people, a hundred customers. Would you expect them all to be worth the same to you?

Of course not. That would be ridiculous.

Just as in life, a small percentage may be family—and the good family too, not the ones you avoid outside of holidays. Others will be your close friends, friends you've had since childhood. And then some will be further out in your circle, and some people you'll hardly know at all. The same is true of your company's customers. Only a handful of your customers will be loyalists, and these loyalists will spend, promote, and defend your company to others.

Generally speaking, you're going to get 80 percent of the value—in life or in business—from 20 percent of those you know. They are going to define your business and your profitability.

From there you have the friends you're happy to see and spend time with but who come and go as circumstances change. Then there are the people you've met out of convenience—maybe because you were the only one who'd pick up the phone at two in the morning when they called—and that's okay too. And from there, eventually, you get to the people where things will never be more than transactional, and others you could have just done without.

Your challenge is figuring out where everyone fits into your business.

If you're like most businesses, you're treating them all the same. Everyone gets the same amount of attention. You're spending the same to reach them. You're giving them all the same promotions. You get just as excited when any one of them responds as any other. You love all of your customers!

We're going to talk about how you find those who are more valuable than all the others combined. The loyalists. They'll remember you—and they expect you to remember them. Not just by welcoming them back by name. Not just by personalizing their emails. That's not enough to make anyone feel loved, never mind the most important people in your life.

It's not enough to learn how to conduct a good conversation. We have to learn how to build relationships too—with the people who matter.

8

KNOWING WHERE THINGS STAND

Whether companies explicitly recognize it or measure it, they are already in relationships with their customers. It's just a question of strength and value—of knowing how important you are to your various customers. Who's a best friend? An acquaintance? A fling? Who are the customers who snapped up that 75 percent–off daily deal, never to return? Who are the long-term, committed partners who haven't been getting the attention from you that they should?

There's actually a way to answer these questions, with the precision that only math can deliver. The metric we use to understand customer relationships is known as customer lifetime value, or CLV. A CLV model predicts how much each of your relationships will be worth over its lifetime. It's quickly becoming the indispensable measure for marketers trying to understand if they are creating sustainable value for their business or merely positioning themselves between transactions.

Calculating Your CLV

The process for calculating CLV is straightforward. So much so that I think of it as following a recipe—a delicious recipe, like baking a chocolate cake or brewing craft beer, if that's your thing. (Since I know nothing about brewing craft beer, we're going with chocolate cake.) I've often found that people have their own recipes for this type of thing—with some very strong feelings attached. The recipe I'm recommending was tested on thousands of customers and found through multiple studies to turn out better than anything else out there.*

---

* Pavel Jasek et al., "Modeling and Application of Customer Lifetime Value in Online Retail," *Informatics* 5, no. 1 (2018): 2; and Shao-Ming Xie and Chun-Yao Huang, "Systematic Comparisons of Customer Base Prediction Accuracy: Pareto/NBD Versus Neural Network," *Asia Pacific Journal of Marketing and Logistics* 33, no. 2 (May 2020).

But I know that's not enough for everyone, and maybe it's not enough for you. So be it. You're going to like what you like when it comes to CLV, so let's get cooking.

1. GATHER THE INGREDIENTS

You'll need only three types of data: the date and value of your transactions* and some type of ID to connect multiple transactions with the same person. I'll refer to that as their name, but it could also mean their customer ID, their email, a loyalty program number—whatever you've got that connects the dots of their purchasing history.

Let's talk about volume: How much data do you need? The greater of twenty-four months or six times the average

ID	Transaction Date	Transaction Value
1234	01/01/2020	$150.00
5678	01/14/2020	$22.00
9012	02/03/2020	$78.00
3456	02/04/2020	$364.00

Figure 8.1

* Some companies use revenue for simplicity's sake, but profit is better.

length of time between transactions. If your customers buy every six months on average, you'll need thirty-six months. You'll split that data, using the first eighteen months to calibrate your model, the next eighteen months to validate it. If you have several years' more data handy, toss it in. If you have less, keep going anyway; the validation test will show how close we come.

2. PUT IT INTO THE OVEN

What goes on inside the CLV model is brilliant but not overly complicated. For simplicity's sake I've built a drag-and-drop, easy-bake online tool for you. Just grab your data and get it in there ...

https://convertedbook.com/clv

... and be ready to catch your cake when it comes out the other side.

In the long run, it's important for every marketer to learn what's happening as things bake so they can own this whole process from end to end. I encourage you to invest the time it will take to learn the models, why they work, and where things can be improved. But right now we're focused on the value—proving they work and making some money. Spoiler: they do work, and you will make money. Don't let success stop you from digging into the research later and learning more.*

3. TAKE OUT YOUR CAKE

If you've chosen to work with a different recipe, so be it. It's your kitchen. But once you pull your cake from the oven, make sure the format of your table looks something like this one:

ID	CLV	Predicted Future Transactions	Average Value per Future Transaction	Probability of Future Transaction
1234	$7,790	82	$95.00	0.99
5678	$5,250	100	$52.50	0.98
9012	$3,850	70	$55.00	0.98
3456	$3,416	28	$122.00	0.95

Figure 8.2

* If you're really interested (overachiever!), the approach we're taking follows the BG/BB and Pareto/NBD models popularized by Peter Fader, the Frances and Pei-Yuan Chia Professor of Marketing at the Wharton School of the University of Pennsylvania, and Bruce Hardie, professor of marketing at the London Business School.

Depending on how you follow my recipe (or your own), you may have more than these five columns. That's fine. We'll ignore them for now.

What you have is a prediction of how your relationship with each customer will unfold. The ID column is simply their name—at least, how you define it in your systems. The CLV column is what we're really focused on: how much value they'll bring to your business. That's the opportunity. It's calculated by multiplying the number of predicted future transactions for the customer by the average value per future transaction. The probability of future transactions is exactly what it sounds like. How likely is this customer to transact with us again? We'll talk about this one later on.

4. TASTE-TEST IT

So how do we know how accurate these predictions are without waiting months or years to see how these relationships actually play out? If we used all our data to build the model, that's exactly what a business would have to do—and that's a tough sell. So, as I mentioned earlier, the model splits the data into halves, using the first as a calibration period to build the model and the

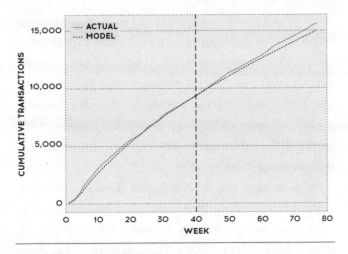

Figure 8.3: Cumulative transactions

second to test its accuracy after it's been constructed. The chart above shows the results, enabling you to compare how the model predicted customers would behave (the dotted line) based on first-half data with the actual behavior from your second-half data (the solid line.)

The dotted line is our predicted result, and the solid line the actual. Sure, we can eyeball the results, but it's better to quantify by measuring the space between the two lines. (Don't reach for your ruler. The model does the math.) If the lines are right on top of each other, the "error rate" is practically zero. The more they diverge, the higher the error rate. The technical term for the overall error rate is the mean average percent error (MAPE, to its friends). If the MAPE exceeds 10 percent overall, then we can't have enough confidence in the quality of the cake to serve it to anybody. It's sad, but you need to dump it in the trash.

Why do some cakes disappoint? Three reasons, usually. The first is insufficient data. You just need to observe a few more customers for a little while longer. The second is poor data quality. The challenge is less about the nasty errors you can detect by sight and more about the extra number that creeps in here or there and can be nearly impossible to detect automatically. Negative values are another perpetual agony—as is the case with returns or loss leaders that exist only to rope in new customers—but they too can be dealt with. Third is a lack of predictability. Some relationships are entirely random and dependent on the customer's fluctuating circumstances because, hey, that's life. Things change. That new job requires a customer to pay for relocation or travel, or a lost job forces them to carry a credit card balance.

For some of you, producing a great-tasting cake will be easier than it is for others. Some of you may have to put in a little more time to get your recipe right. But for almost all of you, it can be done.

5. SLICE IT

We need to take one last step in this process before we give our cake metaphor a well-deserved death. We gathered the ingredients, baked the cake, and did our taste test. Time to serve, right? What do you do? Just toss it to all of your analysts and tell them to grab a fork? No. That's going to be a mess. The tool slices the cake into five pieces, or segments.

Customer Segment	Average Value / Person	Total Value	% of Revenue
1	$3,200	$283,200,000	81%
2	$350	$30,975,000	9%
3	$200	$17,700,000	5%
4	$120	$10,620,000	3%
5	$80	$7,080,000	2%

Figure 8.4

In figure 8.4, 80 percent of the value is coming from the top 20 percent of customers. The bottom fifth will contribute just 5 percent or less. This 80-20 distribution—named the Pareto principle—is how most of these relationships play out. Of course, your distribution may vary. For instance, when it comes to consumer goods like bleach, toothpaste, and gallons of orange juice, the value is spread more widely across the customer segments. The top 20 percent of customers may drive just half of the value. Other industries differ, sometimes dramatically. In mobile applications, Apple finds 95.2 percent of their app store billings will come from just under 8 percent of their customer accounts.*

Grasping—and acting on—your customers' behavior is critical. Regardless of how many segments you use to group your customers, this presentation is the most important way you can share your work with others, allowing them to grasp the same concept: while you may be treating and targeting and spending on all customers equally *today*, your business depends on your relationships with a select few.

* Epic Games, Inc. v. Apple Inc., N.D. Cal., 4:20-cv-05640-YGR, https://app.box.com/s/6b9wmjvr582c95uzma1136exumk6p989 /file/811126940599, slide 20.

Make Sure Your CFO Gets a Piece

Adding up the lifetime value of your individual customers gives you a pretty good estimate of how much your entire customer base is worth to the business, a metric known as customer equity. And CFOs are starting to pay attention. The metric is more credible than the claim that Marketing simply drove every sale that period, while finally recognizing those longer-term investments that are paying off to keep relationships alive and healthy. You've put in the work. Use the results to build your case for a bigger budget, bring the efforts of product and sales teams into closer alignment with yours, and lift the commitment to marketing in your company. You can learn more about putting those happy words into action on the book's website.

*T*his is where everything starts to come together. And with purpose. We're starting simple, with data—the name, transaction value, and date—and then predicting how your customers will behave next. This is an essential and immensely powerful insight: some customers are much more valuable to your business than others.

Take this data and keep it. No. Treasure it. It's going to make you a lot of money as we go on. We're going to use it for a lot more than some simple quintiles going forward, starting with the next lesson. This is just a taste of what's to come. I told you my recipe was delicious. Ready for more?

9

MEET BETTER PEOPLE

Once upon a time, there was a hedge fund analyst who wanted to start an internet company that focused on the quality of his customers. He knew that some people were going to be more valuable to his business over time than others. The question was how to find them, how to bring them into his company, and how to build a great relationship so they'd keep coming back and keep buying. And he found a signal: something that high-net-worth, high-disposable-income individuals in the United States tend to buy more often than people on the opposite end of the spectrum.

Books.

That was part of the brilliance in how Amazon came to be: the confidence of Jeff Bezos that he had found a signal everyone else in retail was overlooking. And he was going to use that signal to gather data on affluent shoppers. To outsiders, his plan made no sense. They thought and talked in transactions: *Books are commodities. They're low margin. You're throwing in free shipping. How are you going to compete with entrenched competition?* In an article in *The New Yorker* in 2017, the writer George Packer described Bezos's rejoinder to a skeptic in this way: "Bezos said that Amazon intended to sell books as a way of gathering data on affluent, educated shoppers. The books would be priced close to cost, in order to increase sales volume. After collecting data on millions of customers, Amazon could figure out how to sell everything else dirt cheap on the internet."*

What that answer reveals is that Bezos thought and talked in relationships. He believed that if he could bring in the people who buy books, deliver an incredible experience, and build great relationships with them, that'd be fantastic. Not because he sold them a book but because he could sell them more and different things later.

---

* George Packer, "Cheap Words," *New Yorker*, February 17–24, 2017.

Not only would he build great bonds with his best customers, but he'd leave lower, less valuable customers for his competitors to fight over.

Relationships take time, and Bezos knew Amazon wouldn't create them overnight. The expectation he set with investors was that he was going to lose money until he set the foundation of the relationships and then expanded them into other categories.

This was the late nineties, and still today, Amazon remains ahead of its competitors. It is fundamentally better at understanding its customers than anybody else is. It listens. It asks questions. Then it puts what it learns to use. If you look at the average lifetime value of an Amazon Prime customer, it's almost thirty times greater than that of an average retailer's customer.*

* Brendan Mathews, "What's a Prime Member Worth to Amazon .com?" *Motley Fool*, February 20, 2018, https://www.fool.com /investing/general/2014/04/21/whats-a-prime-member-worth -to-amazoncom.aspx; and Danny Wong, "How Ecommerce Brands Can Increase Customer Lifetime Value," CM Commerce, March 8, 2017, https://cm-commerce.com/deep-dive/increase-customer-life time-value.

How to Meet Better People

We've talked about how to value your customers by identifying those who matter most—and those who don't—and understanding what those valuations mean for your company. Now the question is how to apply this knowledge to acquire better customers. You'll find that your first-party data—the information your company captures on its own, specific to your business—is going to provide the answers.

As a marketer, there are three ways to build your business. You can meet new people (acquisition). You can improve the relationships you have (development). Or you can work to save relationships that may be on the way out (retention). Let's be clear: most of your effort should go toward acquisition. Finding great relationships—like the customers we've learned to identify—is much easier than trying to change someone into a better person. I know, we're optimists! But it just doesn't happen often or easily. So let's talk about finding more great customers.

TAKE THE NEXT STEP

We'll start with the spreadsheet produced by the recipe we covered in the previous chapter. One by one, column by column, you add new dimensions of behavior to the results. What's the lifetime value of everybody who was acquired by using a coupon code versus those who weren't? Holiday seasons? Website versus mobile app? What if we look at customers by the product category they bought from first? Here's what your first pass might look like.

ID	CLV	Acquisition Channel	Mobile App?	Coupon Code on First Purchase?
1234	$7,790	Paid search	Yes	No
5678	$5,250	Paid search	No	No
9012	$3,850	Social media	No	Yes
3456	$3,416	Affiliate	No	No

Figure 9.1

The purpose of this is to find the characteristics or behaviors of the customers who will be more valuable to you versus less. You can use these insights to create better campaigns, putting more emphasis on the characteristics that lead to better relationships while avoiding those that lead to worse ones.

This is built from first-party data. Owned by your company, it's unique to your company, and it will provide unique insights specific to your customers. You can start to fill in the picture with potential signals that can help answer the question: Who is a high-value customer for your business? Where customers are acquired from is arguably one of the most important characteristics to look at. Was it paid search advertising? Display?

Start with a simple spreadsheet tool, like Microsoft Excel or Google Sheets, and use a pivot table to uncover simple patterns across the data. Nothing complicated. Just enough to prove that you can do it and that your customers behave in identifiably different ways.

Here is one example—and yes, I know, it's a Google example: "On average, customers acquired from Google have a 24% higher lifetime value than customers acquired from other channels. The difference is even larger (27.8%) for those who engaged with Google advertising first and then purchased offline."* Of course, your results may vary.

Now, with some variables—such as mobile app downloads or loyalty programs—there's going to be the question of whether you really expected these platforms or programs to drive more value in the first place. Did you build the mobile app because you expected it to drive sales or because you wanted to have a place on your customer's phone, be able to drop a message on their home screen at a moment's notice? What about your loyalty program? Is it really building more profitable relationships, or just recognizing behavior that would have occurred anyway? If the answer is that you expected these things to drive higher lifetime values and they're not, it may be worth reassessing your strategy. Here's a sample report looking at how the average CLV changes based on how the customer was acquired:

---

* Tat Y. Chan, Ying Xie, and Chunhua Wu, "Measuring the Lifetime Value of Customers Acquired from Google Search Advertising," *Marketing Science* 30, no. 5 (September–October 2011): 837–50.

Acquisition Channel	Average Initial Transaction Value	Average CLV
Paid Search	$80	$6,400
Display	$360	$1,280
Email Marketing	$95	$2,000
Affiliate	$480	$800
Video	$410	$4,500
Unknown/Other	$65	$3,050

Figure 9.2

Marketers who are studying individual interactions tend to look only at the first two columns. They'll ask, "Where did people come from?" and "How much did they spend today?" They'd look at only the first two columns in the chart above, see that the average transaction value of affiliate marketing is highest, and draw the obvious conclusion: "I'm putting all my money there."

But what the third column reveals is that, while these people spend a lot on their first transaction, there's not much residual value left. They spend a lot today, then they're gone. They're not going to contribute a lot to your business overall. Acquiring more of these customers is a suboptimal strategy.

For this retailer, paid search is a different story. These customers spend a lot less on their initial transaction but generally spend a lot more going forward. Almost eight times as much, to be precise about it. They're a much better investment.

I'm not saying that's sure to be the case for you. Your numbers will tell their own story.

DON'T BE SHY

Remember: you're not limited to the data you already have. Early on, we talked about the importance of asking questions in the context of a conversation with your customers. Ask what attributes customers find most important in your brand. Do your high-CLV customers value your service the most? The awesome selection? Maybe shipping time? Sometimes companies use surveys, which we covered in chapter 3. Net Promoter Score, or NPS, is a common one: "On a scale of zero to ten, how likely are you to recommend our business to a friend or a colleague?" Your goal is to determine how closely their enthusiasm ties to what happens next.

TRUST YOUR EXPERIENCE

You found your most valuable customers. You figured out a bunch of reasons why you connect so well. How much is this knowledge worth to your business? Absolutely nothing—until you put it to use.

Using a list of email addresses of your valuable customers, many ad networks, including Google, can use signals to craft ad campaigns that reach more people like them. You did all the heavy lifting when you calculated the CLVs of your customers, so you owe it to yourself to take this trivial step to put those results to use. Just give yourself enough room to work. If your list is filled with only your very best relationships, there may not be enough people in the market to meet those expectations. Start with a wider net—say, the top 25 percent of your customers—to get the volume first.

LET INTERESTS GUIDE YOU

Here's the rub with the first approach. It's incredibly simple, but you won't be taking advantage of your most valuable asset: your data. You're just telling Google, "Hey! I like this person," and letting them work their magic from what *they* know. But they can't have the same understanding that comes from being in an actual relationship with that person, whether it's knowing the products they bought or the campaigns they clicked on. All of those insights that you started to gather from the first part of this exercise can (and should) be weighted into your campaigns. Nothing dramatic. Spend a little more aggressively on campaigns that target the positive signals in a relationship, less on the weaker ones, validating as you go.

FOCUS ON THEIR POTENTIAL

Every time you begin a new customer relationship, you predict its value. If you want ad networks to provide the best recommendations for new and better customers, share this data with them too. Otherwise, your friends (we hope) at the ad networks won't know whom to introduce you to next. Get this done by updating the value you send back to your ad network, commonly known as your conversion value. Most marketers send the value of individual transactions—that single, immediate purchase. The savvy ones are starting to provide lifetime value— the long-term value to their business—instead.

Which option is my recommendation? Targeting a similar audience, the first option, wins by virtue of its simplicity. The second option, targeting by attribute, is more challenging, since you need to answer the question of *why* customers are valuable instead of just *who* is valuable. But for potentially larger audiences and deeper insights—the products they love, the behaviors they share—to guide you forward, the third option, updating conversion values to CLV, is where you want to end up. But it's not the place to start. Better to start simple, learn, and build from there.

TRY THE OPPOSITE

Remember, everything works in reverse. Just as you can find the characteristics that identify your high-value customers, you can find those that identify—and exclude—the worst. No need to deliberately end those relationships; the customers are still spending *something*, after all. Just make sure they aren't taking up too much of your attention, relative to what they're giving back. That effort and money are better spent elsewhere.

A word of caution: don't throw all your dollars into chasing more high-value customers, not right away. Start by spending *slightly* more on valuable customers and *slightly* less on the less valuable ones. Learn how customers respond, ensure that your efforts are paying off—and keep a cushion for risk.

Tips for Meeting the Ones That Matter

TRUST FIRST IMPRESSIONS

You may have too much data on your customers. Or too little. Where do you start from? My suggestion is to start from the first interaction, the first date. Behaviors in those moments—everything from the product categories they purchased from to the season during which they were acquired to their use of promotional codes—can generally give you a sense of where things are going after that. As Oscar Wilde put it: "My first impressions of people are invariably right."*

JUDGE OTHERS BY THEIR ACTIONS

In the old days of catalog marketing, there was only so much information you could gather on your customers. You couldn't see how many times they opened your catalog, where they turned first, where they were sitting. Marketers relied on demographics to do their targeting.

* Oscar Wilde, *The Importance of Being Earnest*, act 2.

And demographics are real; they're familiar. It's why marketers love to create personas: *Here's Jane. She's thirty-four, newly married with two kids, and loves wearing Lululemon when she pedals her Peloton in the middle of the living room.*

Behavioral characteristics are so much more boring. *Here's Cecilia. She came to our site eleven times before ordering.*

But here's reality: behavioral attributes (the product purchased, times visiting the site) have much more value than demographics (age, gender, household income). There's nothing wrong with creating personas, but if they're focused on demographics, they're focused on the wrong thing.

Go to the data. Look at what your customers are actually doing and actually buying.

MAKE IT TOOL TIME

You may get to a point where your spreadsheet is no longer manageable when trying to wrap your head around thousands of different but interconnected signals. After you've explored all of the easy answers, you may find yourself up against the roadblock of *How does this scale?*

For some companies, we return to that answer of

machine learning. Computers can grind and crunch data faster than mere human analysts can. Machine learning can be automated, and it can reveal patterns you might miss, as well as patterns that change. With some tools capturing over one hundred thousand signals on your website alone, there's no looking at those by hand. Balancing the power of this knowledge are the limits of practical value in what you learn. The thrill of finding that nuanced insight of how every customer who purchased your product at full price during December on their mobile device in California and took advantage of free shipping has super high CLV may be undetectable because few other customers meet this pattern. Thus, machine learning doesn't recognize the value of this behavior.

Still, the benefits of machine learning can be significant and, at a certain point, necessary. Just don't make the mistake of thinking you need to start with it, no matter what that well-funded start-up tells you about its magic black box. Prove that you can acquire new, high-value customers through simple segmentation first, before engaging in more complex techniques.

What we've been talking about here is looking at all your customers and figuring out what makes the best of them special, and then finding more of them. We do the same thing when it comes to making friends. We look at our past relationships and think, Well, I loved these qualities in them but hated those. *And with time we learn to gravitate toward the people we get along well with. In the world of marketing, you're applying the same dynamic— and it's the single most important thing you need to do. But it's not the only thing.*

10

ACCEPT PEOPLE FOR WHO THEY ARE

A million guys walk into a Silicon Valley bar.

No one buys anything.

Bar declares massive success.

It's an apocryphal story become a well-worn joke.

But this aspiring unicorn company was different. It had all the right pieces. Its customers would spend, on average, $550 over their lifetime but were being acquired for a mere fraction of that, just over four bucks. Well-funded investors added gasoline to the fire. Acquisitions surged into the beloved hockey-stick growth. The visionary CEO painted word pictures of redefining humanity with his amazing management team and their army of customers.

What followed was a fire sale. The unicorn's valuation was 98 percent lower the following year, and for investors the joke was no longer funny.

I retraced the steps with the help of an ousted executive and a few pints of beer, and what emerged was a cautionary tale with a lesson grounded more in empathy—it could happen to anyone—than in stupidity.

The investors set the growth targets. Aggressive, but manageable. As the company picked through one customer segment after the next, its product wasn't always a perfect fit, but it was sellable. Customer acquisition costs (CAC) grew exponentially, peaking close to $200, but plenty of value should have remained.

The alarm came from a prebuilt report, routinely generated and regularly overlooked: What percentage of sales were coming from new versus returning customers? New customers were buying—that was the work of the acquisition budget, the ads and promotions—but most were never seen again.

This was a cautionary tale of lifetime value. Did you catch the clue in the beginning? The company was using an *average* value of $550. In its strategy and its pitch deck, all customers were worth that amount, regardless of who they were or how they were acquired. But in practice, a small fraction were worth significantly more and the vast majority worth much, much less. You know that now; they didn't then. That $200 CAC was far more than many of their customers were worth.

With ample money in the bank and the goodwill of the board, they surged forward with a turnaround and committed the real sin of CLV: they tried to turn low-value customers into top spenders, lead into gold.

Acquisition efforts came to a halt. All hands on deck to win their existing customers back. More money. More marketing. More promotions. Margins lost as a sacrifice.

Some customers bit. Most didn't. In the end, the company sold what was left, largely a customer list and some excess inventory.

Why You Can't Count on People to Change

It's no surprise that many companies believe in their ability to develop brilliant, profitable relationships with any customer, as long as they can get them through the door. *They will see how great the company really is for them, if*

*only they can get that chance. Give them coupons! Give them
free shipping! Whatever it takes to bring them in.* We saw
this in the daily deals space years ago. Restaurants, bak-
eries, and yoga classes drew hordes of customers for $5
each, eating the cost with hopes of turning them into
high-value customers later. Most never came back. They
were interested in the deal, not the relationship.

It's the wrong way for any company to think of its
customers. Gathering a whole bunch of customers and
then trying to make them valuable is *incredibly hard.*
Changing a customer's behavior is almost the same
thing as changing a person—trying to change them into
your soul mate through effort and determination when
it just isn't meant to be. There are some things you can
do that will improve your likelihood of success in moving them, say, from the bottom tier to the next rung up.
(We'll get to those in just a bit.) But you're not going to
get them to the top. Don't make it central to your growth
plans to do so. The road to business oblivion is littered
with dead companies that did.

In a 2011 study, researchers called attention to the difficulty of running a successful cross-selling campaign.*

---

* Shibo Li, Baohong Sun, and Alan L. Montgomery, "Cross-Selling the
Right Product to the Right Customer at the Right Time," *Journal of
Marketing Research* 48, no. 4 (August 2011): 683–700.

"The average response rate as measured by a customer purchase within three months after a cross-selling campaign is approximately 2 percent," they wrote. That's a waste of effort, an exercise in the pursuit of mediocrity... or worse.

So is there anything that the unicorn could have done differently?

You bet. They should have identified and respected differences in how customers will behave and spend. Averages are grossly misleading, and in this case were the source of the company's poor decisions. Once they recognized their original sin, they could have corrected their acquisition efforts to focus on finding more people like the high-value customers they had attracted. Instead, they did the opposite, committing a second sin: they tried to turn terrible relationships into great ones, a futile pursuit that few survive.

Successful companies understand the behaviors of their best customers and build acquisition campaigns to meet those behaviors. Even they acquire poor customers, much as they hope to avoid them. It's reality: sometimes we find people in our lives whom we'd prefer we hadn't met. I'm not saying you shouldn't try to make the most of these customers. My point is that you need to be realistic about how much (and how little) they'll change and invest accordingly. Let's talk about how.

How to Change People as Much as You Can

GIVE YOUR BEST ADVICE

There is no more powerful signal than a purchase. The customer committed. Make the most of that moment. Recommendation engines can derive slightly more value from each purchase by up-sizing the transaction: larger sizes, greater quantities, supplemental products. You bought the little toy train; don't forget the batteries! One study found that Amazon's recommendations are responsible for more than 35 percent of their revenue, yet more than half of retailers don't use them.* Seventy-five percent of Netflix viewing is driven by recommendations.

Don't limit yourself to on-site conversations, either.

* Ian MacKenzie, Chris Meyer, and Steve Noble, "How Retailers Can Keep Up with Consumers," McKinsey & Company, October 1, 2013.

You can be proactive in making recommendations through email campaigns and display advertising too. As long as those recommendations are relevant to the customer, they won't undermine your larger relationship. There is evidence that promoting supplemental products—even as much as forty-eight hours after the initial sale—can still prove effective.

FIND MORE TO OFFER

This is the go-to solution for ambitious businesses: they look for new stuff to sell, complementary stuff that leverages their relationships with their current customers. Mature firms with clear, set product offerings aren't always as nimble—but that's not to say that they can't or shouldn't try to sell new stuff too. Our calculations for lifetime value assume that a customer will never change, that they'll always be the same person, and that they can't grow as a customer in response to new products and services. If you sell only furniture, you're calculating the lifetime value for everyone who buys furniture. But what if you sold TVs too? The insurance giant Allstate even found that it was four times more effective to cross-sell existing customers on new insurance products than it was to acquire new customers.* If that bar in Silicon Valley is going to have any success, it's going to have to start cross-selling some honey-barbecue wings.

DON'T ENCOURAGE EVERYONE

If you do decide to develop customer relationships, don't do it for everyone. You need to look for signals that identify whom to target—and whom to avoid, those who cost too much to service. (We'll find the same theme applies in retention too, where we're headed next. But let's not get ahead of ourselves.)

Research points to the upside in this dynamic: how identifying factors like the time between purchases, the ratio of product returns, and the category of an initial purchase can be used to greatly improve the effectiveness of cross-selling by targeting better customers.†

And the downside, focusing on the wrong people? Another study found that while cross-selling is, in the

---

* Pamela Moy, "Not Just for Newbies: Use Digital to Nurture Your Existing High-Value Customers," Think with Google, June 2017.
† V. Kumar, Morris George, and Joseph Pancras, "Cross-Buying in Retailing: Drivers and Consequences," *Journal of Retailing* 84, no. 1 (April 2008): 15–27.

aggregate, profitable, one in every five customers will actually cost you money. The price of encouraging these people is high, accounting for 70 percent of all money-losing transactions.* "The more cross-buying an unprofitable customer does, the greater the loss," the study said.

Remember our discussion around asking questions? Refine your approach by asking about share of wallet: *Say, Gopi, how much do you spend on travel every year?* (Or books, or cold-brew coffee, whatever it is.) If you're getting just a small slice of Gopi's spend, there may be an opportunity to grow and deepen that relationship; if you've already got it all, not so much.

---

* Denish Shah and V. Kumar, "The Dark Side of Cross-Selling," *Harvard Business Review*, December 2012.

No one wants to embody the Silicon Valley bar joke. Avoiding that fate begins with spending most of your time on acquiring great customers. It's a lot easier to do that than it is to try to change an existing customer for the better. That said, there are things you can do to make your existing relationships a little more valuable. Don't get carried away; you're not going to take a terrible relationship and make it one of your best. But you can take someone who's great and nudge them in the right direction. Your average customers you can get to spend a little more. Don't let your optimism override good judgment. Make the most of the opportunities that are right in front of you—and then move on.

11

MAKE IT WORK OR SAY GOODBYE

When it comes to forging lifelong relationships, customer retention is the glue. It makes everything else work. The valet who found a guest's left-behind passport and rushed off to catch her at the airport now has a customer who's not just staying in the same hotel the next time she's in town but evangelizing for it with a glowing review on Tripadvisor. The retail store that took the return on a product purchased on the discount rack decades ago, no questions asked, now has a loyal shopper who's first in line for the new season's clothes at full price. My wife once sent her pet-food orders to her mother's home in Chicago instead of ours outside San Francisco. "Don't worry about it," customer service said. "We'll refund you the money. Have your mom donate the products to a local animal shelter." We've been ordering from that retailer exclusively ever since.

Try not to smile at that story. I dare you. Of course you're smiling. Everyone loves those stories. And every company I meet with agrees that retention is really important. But when I tell them how the best companies approach retention, I get sad eyes around the table: *If only we were as big as they are; if only we had their margins; if only we could afford to do what they do.*

It's not size that matters, or margins. The masters of retention are just using their data better. They're distinguishing the customers worth saving from those who aren't, and they're doing that based not on the margin of a single transaction but on their lifetime value.

Amazon's digital video service, known today as Amazon Prime Video, proactively refunds customers for their movie rentals when they detect that the viewing experience wasn't up to their standards.* They don't worry

---

* https://www.sec.gov/Archives/edgar/data/1018724/000119312513 151836/d511111dex991.htm. If you follow the link, you'll see that the service was initially called Amazon Video on Demand. So literal!

about the $2.99 they're losing on the product, as most companies do. Amazon is notorious for taking the longer view. They recognize that if they don't intervene, you're gone for good, so they act to save the relationship, even if the issue is not their service but your bandwidth.

Then there are the airlines.* You may earn the most precious status of loyalty tiers, but that won't determine their answer when you ask them to waive a change fee. They assign a score based on how much value you're expected to bring to the relationship and, more important, your risk of leaving. Fly often enough from San Francisco to New York City, a lucrative and competitive route, and they're going to do all they can to keep you on their planes and not someone else's. Fly to their hub, because it's your only way to get there, and you can sit back and enjoy your seat in coach. They know they'll see you again the next time.

---

* Gary Leff, "How American Airlines Scores Its Customers," *View from the Wing*, November 3, 2018; Jeff Edwards, "American's Top-Secret Passenger Ratings May Come to Light," *flyertalk*, November 12, 2019.

Why You Need to Focus on What's at Stake

If I screw up something with my wife, I might pick up a bouquet of market flowers or prepare a classic Bolognese. I'll do this even if it was absolutely, 100 percent not my fault.

Seriously. It wasn't!

I *think*?

In truth it doesn't matter. The relationship is *that* important and I've learned that I still miss signals. But an acquaintance? A call of apology, maybe even less: a text, if it has been a while since we last spoke.

You can't treat all your customers as commodities, any more than you would your friends or family. That'd be a disaster. But your relationships with your valuable customers matter much more to you than the rest. Distinguish between the two. Always look for signals that something might be going wrong—but base your actions on what's at stake for your company.

The market is moving in this direction. As your competitors recognize and strengthen their approach, it raises the expectations of consumers. The Amazon video example comes from a letter Jeff Bezos wrote to his shareholders in 2012, explaining why the company was so successful. They've undoubtedly improved their retention practices since. How about you?

How to Know When to Intervene

LOOK FOR THE LUGGAGE

Start by looking for a sign that something is wrong. Specific website signals, such as turning off an auto-renew program or visiting a support page on account cancellations, are as strong as they come. But they're also the same as someone standing at the entryway, bags in hand, declaring it's over. Saving that relationship is an uphill battle. Seek other signs: lower service usage, fewer website visits, decreased email open rate. Companies will also look at increasing time between orders.

A second option is to take a modeling approach, as we discussed in chapter 8. You can use machine learning and data to identify the signals that point to the customer relationships with the most promise—and you can use the same technique to identify those at risk as well. Connecting all of the individual dots is more effective than any one discrete signal. She hasn't returned my call yet. Is that a problem or not? Models have a better chance of taking everything else that's happened in the relationship into consideration.

You've got a third option too, a middle ground, if you use the chocolate cake recipe I shared for calculating customer lifetime value. The value in this approach is that it gives companies an objective way to judge whether someone is actually a customer or not. Many companies count as customers anyone who looks their way, by signing up for a newsletter or making a purchase once, back in the age of steam. Others are more selective but arbitrary. Did the person buy in the past twelve months? How about the past twenty-four months? Does that count?

The model I shared produces a column of data—known as probability of future transaction—that says, *Based on what we've already observed, what's the likelihood that this customer is going to purchase again?* The model does the heavy lifting, and the results are tied to every one of your customers. It can say 90 percent. It can say 10 percent. Maybe there's not even a relationship to begin with. Every week when you run the model, it gives you an updated number. You can see both the trends and even when a single relationship might be veering off course. (I told you it was a great recipe.)

WEIGH YOUR CHANCES

Of all the customers who are sending worrisome signals, trending in the wrong direction, which should you intervene with? For most marketers, the answer is simple: "Whoever is about to leave!" But trying to save every customer is the wrong approach. Think of it from the relationship point of view. If someone hates you and says they're never going to talk to you again, what are the odds of turning that around? Maybe you can do it. But it's going to take a lot more effort than reaching out to a good friend who's gone silent for a while.

You should intervene only with the customers whom you want to stay. Seems obvious enough, right? But here's the nuance. It's also not enough to ask, "Who's going to leave?" The next question is just as important: "Do we want them to stay?" If your business intervenes, will you recover the costs of keeping that relationship, or are you simply making yourself feel better that you lost one less person this quarter? There's this too, even with the best of relationships: sometimes it's goodbye. There's always an end point, even with your most valuable customers. It's painful to say it, but it's true. Love hurts. Say your customer has a lifetime value of $1,000, and that's high for your company. When they've spent $990 with you, the relationship is all but over. You don't get anywhere by trying to squeeze out that last $10 and hold on to them for a couple more months. Yes, there's always a chance they'll surprise you and buy something more. But if you're chasing those last dollars, you're investing in the wrong people. When a relationship runs its course, you need to be comfortable walking away. Hey, it's been a lot of fun! You've captured all the value you can. Time to move on.

Some companies take an aggressive stance. They strike first and fire their bad customers. "They're weighing down the business. They're taking up our support channels. We're closing the door."

Most evidence says this is the worst thing you can do, from both a business and a public relations perspective. Customers are going to come, and they're going to spend with you—and even if it's only a few dollars, be okay with it. They're still your customers, after all. But you shouldn't listen to them as much or service them in the same ways. Save some money on advertising, and don't work aggressively to keep them.

CHOOSE: FLOWERS OR HANDSHAKES

Once you've answered the *who*, you need to test the *how*. How are you going to retain these valuable customers? Keep in mind that simple interventions work. One study found that a men's hair salon loyalty program with a modest reward—a $5-off coupon for every $100 spent— increased the lifetime value of its customers by 29 percent.* More than 80 percent of that improvement came from improved retention, even though the coupon redemption rate was low. These findings blew people's minds. They suggest that emotional rather than economic factors drive results. So start small, and don't give away the store.

Don't settle on just one intervention, either; different people will respond to different interventions, so it's important to test an array of ideas. Adjust as you learn how customers respond—and remember: don't test with only the customers who are most likely to leave.

Let's say you went after your certain-to-leave cus-

* Arun Gopalakrishnan et al., "Can Non-Tiered Customer Loyalty Programs Be Profitable?" *Marketing Science* 40, no. 3 (March 2021): 508–26, https://doi.org/10.1287/mksc.2020.1268.

tomers, the ones with a 95 percent chance or higher of not coming back. You throw them an offer of free shipping on their next order. But they're really unhappy with you; they're not taking that. Okay. You try something more aggressive: $20 off on your next order! And that's more successful. Some buy again. And you think, *Success! We had to give away a little more, but we kept those customers!*

But what if you shared the offer with a bunch of customers with a 70 percent chance of leaving, rather than a 95 percent chance? What if the free shipping offer to them would have worked just fine? Research suggests you missed that opportunity, because you didn't intervene until the threat to your relationship was deeper—and then you had to give them more.

*M*ost companies accept that they need a retention strategy, but learning how to develop an effective program requires skill. It's not enough to wait until the customer hits the eject button—CANCEL MY ACCOUNT. You need to be able to identify a sign that tells you they're at risk. I've given you a couple you can test with. And when it comes to retaining customers, as with acquiring them, don't treat everyone equally. Be deliberate and precise in whom you target, and how. Don't slam the door on any of your customers. But don't break out the good whiskey for all of them, either.

12

LISTEN TO THE RIGHT VOICES

One of my first projects at Google involved scrutinizing billions of ad impressions to figure out the rules—the best practices—for making someone click the ad. That was 2011, and twenty or so of the conclusions we reached—insights around building provocative calls to action, improving ad recall, and establishing new brand awareness—are still considered best practices today.

It's not a great legacy.

The problem isn't the conclusions I reached. It's the methodology behind them. Everything was equal. A click was a click. A sale was a sale. You know the problem: not all clicks and not all sales are equal.

Imagine you ran a survey and found that 87 percent of respondents said the most important thing about air travel is low fares.* The other 13 percent valued seat comfort and service. Every answer being equal, you'd build your marketing around low fares. But what if you also knew that 87 percent flew only once each year? And that the 13 percent, your frequent fliers, generated 50 percent of your revenue? Your click-through rate might tell you that your campaign is doing well on average. But are those frequent fliers average? Are they just part of the crowd, or do they stand out from it?

That's the lesson. Anything you build, whether it's a creative landing page, ad copy, an email campaign, or a brand, must be built with consideration for the relationships it fosters. High- and low-value customers prefer different things, whether it's speaking to the legacy of the brand, the durability of the products, or simply that something is 75 percent off for today only. We've even seen differences in what high-value customers prefer across different businesses in the same category.

* Actually, we don't need to imagine it. David Yanofsky, "Half of American Airlines' Revenue Came from 13% of Its Customers," *Quartz*, October 27, 2015.

Why You Need to Listen to Some and Ignore Others

You're struggling and in search of advice. You can ask your partner or a parent for their opinion. Your friends may offer theirs. Maybe you even ask that Uber driver who seemed okay with your venting on the way back from the airport. Would everyone's opinion be equal? Whose opinion matters more? This is where you start to connect the pieces. You know how to identify, develop, and retain the high-value customers, but the messaging—what's coming out of your mouth—needs to align with their expectations. That begins with listening to them until you understand what they're looking for and the language they speak. If you're talking with affluent people, they're probably going to care less about value and costs and more about quality and service. If you're talking with hard-core gamers, they may engage more with messaging that doesn't appeal to a mainstream audience. The point is that it's not enough just to target high-value customers; what you say has to resonate with them too. Otherwise it's a disappointing mismatch and it's not going to last.

Customer Segment	Email Open Rate Version 1	Email Open Rate Version 2
Top 20%	8.0%	3.0%
2nd best 20%	2.2%	3.0%
3rd best 20%	2.0%	3.0%
4th best 20%	2.0%	5.0%
Bottom 20%	2.0%	6.0%
Average	3.2%	4.0%

Figure 12.1

In this example, companies that look at all customer relationships as being equal will deduce that version 2 had the strongest performance, with a higher average open rate. However, by focusing on engagement with high-CLV customers, the opposite conclusion is reached. Version 1 is going to capture the specific attention of customers who will contribute the most value back to the business. Whom would you want to attract?

It's time to build your new set of best practices. One that considers the long-term value of the customers you want to reach, not just whether or not they've purchased something, at some point, from your business. It's not calculating lifetime value or targeting more customers with ads that elevates you into a customer-centric business. It's this lesson. Right here: let your insights shape who you listen to and how your actions speak.

The fact is that the best companies are aggressively trying to understand the best approaches for engaging high-value customers. To speak to them in a new way that is lost when optimizing to the average. There are no shortcuts. Your customers are *yours*.

How to Listen to the Ones You Love

There are no mysteries to this, either. For every campaign or experiment you run, weigh the impact alongside the lifetime value of the customers it reached. Was it bringing in people you'd see again or people lost forever after the pop-up sale ends? Would you have fewer game downloads but more people who would buy those sweet, pure-profit expansion packs? You already put in the effort to calculate everyone's lifetime value. This puts it to use. It's time to write your company's new rule book.

Three things to keep in mind:

---

1. **You need a slightly larger sample size for these tests.** When you're looking past the average, you're going to want large enough segments of each group, high- and low-value customers, as well as everyone in between. It's important to make sure that what you hear is representative of the group.

2. **Don't define the highest-value customers too narrowly.** Start with the top quarter. You're still talking about friends you want to keep. It gives you a larger group to experiment with. You'll start learning, and you'll start getting better.

3. **Be sure to learn as much as you can about your low-value customers, so you know what to avoid.** It could be you're bringing in low-value customers because you're putting out a message like "Buy our really cheap product!"

Work backward too. It's like reflecting on your experiences in life. Don't just look forward, learning from the new data you generate. If you have data available from previous experiments—at the individual customer level—why not analyze those results from the point of view of maximizing lifetime value instead of one-off transactions? Would you have made a different decision based on what you see? We can't change the past, but we can learn from it and apply its lessons in the future.

Finally, share your insights across the company. There'll be implications in what you find for product development, service, and sales that are all in pursuit of the same objectives—more money, more growth. Zappos found that its most valuable customers had the highest return rate.* The action? A 365-day return policy with free shipping both ways. The margins and frequent purchases more than offset the return cost for this high-value group. Arm everyone with what you've learned, and you'll nudge them toward practices that emphasize the customers who matter most.

---

* Addy Dugdale, "Zappos' Best Customers Are Also the Ones Who Return the Most Orders," *Fast Company,* April 13, 2010.

*M*arketing used to be entirely about clicks. Get someone to click + get someone to buy = success. Then move on. That's not so much wrong as outdated. The best companies today are playing a longer game. They're focused on their most valuable customers, and they're bringing that focus to their products, their marketing, and their service. They're becoming better at grabbing the high-value customers and convincing them to stay. Those who don't move in this direction will be left behind.

13

GET OUT THERE

ny understanding we have of great—or punishing—relationships is limited to the experiences we've gathered. If you've sold only one type of product, it's challenging to know how new categories could expand your relationships. If you've built campaigns only around immediate, one-time "buy it now or our marketing was wasted" objectives, it's going to be harder to see the opportunity that more committed relationships can bring. We've talked about this already, when we introduced the value of machine learning in chapter 5. Opportunities are biased toward existing strategies and metrics. Exploration is the way you open those horizons.

What you're doing now is a starting point. You owe it to your business to capture data about other opportunities and other places you could go to meet more great customers. There are likely new customers out there who you haven't reached, customers who would welcome long-term relationships with your company. The marketing channels they use and the product categories they want to purchase may make more sense for you than ever, now that you understand their full value.

Any marketer can apply the principles we've talked about to refine their business. Extraordinary marketers will see this as a starting point, as an opportunity to ask new questions, learn new lessons, and start building better long-term relationships with the customers who matter most.

This is it—the entire secret, the entire strategy: you're not confined only to what your business is doing today.

Hey, we ran a campaign. Everyone loves the shiny red car!

Okay. What about our most valuable customers?

No, they like the blue truck.

Okay! Which one should we run?

Be curious. Imagine what you can do. And go do it.

PART 3

SELF-IMPROVEMENT

14

LET'S TALK ABOUT YOU

I hope a great deal has changed since we started this journey together. The once-confident understanding of a single transaction—the $450 pair of shoes—has given way to a deeper story about the necessity of conversation and the unadulterated optimism that there's a relationship to find underneath the piles of money you invested, for the shoe shopper and all of the other customers who might be otherwise lost in your CRM system. You're starting to get that confidence, that swagger. Tomorrow is going to be a better day—and the day after, even better.

But there's still one thing standing in your way: If you're working alone, the lessons you've learned may not be enough. You are part of a larger organization filled with people who haven't shared in these lessons. They have their own ways of making decisions. Their own ways of testing. Their own processes and forms of proof. Their own incentives, their own turf to defend, their own fears at night. And this is going to limit the change you can make by yourself.

How do you help to guide and bring other people in your organization along on this same journey of learning? How do you create space in your own organization to have the conversations and build the relationships of understanding that will advance your company's interests, and your own? Well, you should share this book with them. They'll read it and join you on the journey. (Hopefully.) And then keep reading, because we're going to discuss a few ways you can take these challenges head-on together.

15

TAKE SMALL STEPS FORWARD

In our nation's capital, bribing is not allowed—at least not publicly. For years the lobbyists on K Street would win time with elected officials by taking them out for dinner. Offer them a free dry-aged rib eye, and their attention was yours for the next few hours. A cozy arrangement that led to a glut of steak houses within a few blocks of the Capitol.

In 2007, Congress was compelled to act. The only question was how. You could say no dinners, but then they'd just do lunch. No lunch? Breakfast. What about hors d'oeuvres?

Aha!

The result was known by its friends as the toothpick rule.

While meals were out altogether, an exception was carved out for "food that you have to eat standing up using a toothpick."* The first time I held a measurement workshop for some government officials in our Washington, DC, office, we actually had someone come down from Legal to ensure that all of our snacks were in compliance. Our lawyers actually have a slightly stricter interpretation of the rules—"nothing greater than 1 inch by 1 inch in size" and, my personal favorite, "self-supporting." So, yes, they brought a ruler and tried to knock over the food.

You know where this is headed.

There's now an entire industry of people, a "toothpick industry," dedicated to finding different ways to work with and bend the rules:

> "We had to get very clever with food-delivery devices that [held items] substantive enough so that if somebody ate enough of them, it could make up a full meal," said Mark Michael of Occasions

---

* Brody Mullins, "No Free Lunch: New Ethics Rules Vex Capitol Hill," *Wall Street Journal*, January 29, 2007.

Caterers. . . . Over the years, this has included 40 kinds of sticks, from meat skewers to bamboo spears to dessert lollipops.*

It's absurd, right? A case study in why Washington can be an incredibly frustrating place. You look at it, and it's entirely crazy. Government inefficiency in action.

Until you take a step back and think about the goal, the original intention of the rule: the goal was to reduce lobbyist influence on politicians. They were going out to too many dinners.

Based on that objective alone, did it work? Yes. It stopped them from going to dinners and eliminated work-arounds on meals altogether, and it provided guidelines as to what's acceptable. We've gone from three-hour steak dinners to cubes on a toothpick. It did what it set out to do.

Is it perfect? Absolutely not. But it's a step forward. It's progress.

* Britt Peterson, "How a Tiny Splinter of Wood Keeps Congress Clean," *Washingtonian*, March 3, 2016.

Why Small Is Beautiful

By this point, I hope we can all agree that it would not be a good idea to sit at home on your couch and try to think of the perfect thing to say to somebody when you go out that night. Do that and you're not going out. You're going to be sitting in your basement for a long, long time. It's a lot easier to say, *Is there something I could learn from my previous experiences about what* not *to do tonight?* Just one thing, that's all.

I like the toothpick story because it makes a powerful point. Too many companies get stuck on their couch whenever they're trying to develop a new program, a new strategy, a new interpretation of data. They want everything to be perfect. They get lost in all the reasons they think it won't work or is incomplete. They don't move forward until the data sparkles, until it's collected with no bias, until the models are proven and validated in every possible condition. So they do nothing at all.

This is where start-ups stand out. Most are comfortable knowing they don't have all the data, all the answers. They're not supposed to. They're scrappy, they're underfunded, they're working out of someone's garage. And they're okay with it. They just need to keep moving until they prove the viability of their business. They'll take the 90 percent solution—and so will the best businesses in the world. It sets them apart from their competitors, the billion-dollar conglomerates that believe with their resources, size, and people, they're entitled to perfect data. Their standards are higher, but in fact it's generally harder for them to extract good data through the webs of bureaucracy.

How to Think Small

Deep breath! Lower your expectations. Seek progress, not perfection. Trust that small, iterative changes will lead you forward.

I'm happy to acknowledge that the CLV formula I recommended in baking our chocolate cake will not produce the best chocolate cake in the world. All I'm saying is that it's the best chocolate cake I've tasted so far. Is there a chance you could bake something better? Yes. I encourage you to undertake that pursuit—but I don't want you to say you're not baking anything until you figure it out. Don't get lost in nuance; make progress.

Even small changes in marketing strategy bring risk. Guaranteed changes are often boring and uninspired and don't lead to higher sales. We'll talk to lots of market-ers who'll say, "Look, this costs $50,000, so I don't want to try it until I have enough evidence to make sure it's the right direction. Let me spend a few months figuring this out." What they don't consider is that by not taking that $50,000 risk, they could be missing out on a million dol-lars in sales. They don't look at the opportunity cost of inaction, of staying home one more night on their couch. Instead, they look only at what they're putting on the table. There are two sides to the coin of risk—so flip it.

As soon as the powers that be in Washington imposed the toothpick rule, it became clear that more work needed to be done. A rule intended to stop lobbyists from buying lawmakers big, juicy steaks did its job—but then the industry adapted. Now the powers that be need to do the same.

I'm not saying this to discourage you. My point is that even the most brilliant idea won't work forever. Maybe you've figured out the best pickup line ever; you say it to someone and they instantly fall in love with you. But if you've come up with anything that great, chances are other people will figure it out too. After a couple months, all you are is unoriginal, because everyone else is saying the same thing. The market will change. Your customers will change. And the process of being better never ends.

A lot of marketers try to find perfect solutions to their problems, which actually impedes their progress. If they'd been trying to bring the lobbyists' steak house strategy under control, they wouldn't have rolled out a new piece of legislation until they were sure they had closed every loophole. This mindset underestimates the impact of small changes. An imperfect step is less attractive, less sexy. But the truth is that big fixes are few and far between. It's more productive to focus on what you can do each day to make your marketing practices slightly better. These modest improvements add up—but they're the sort of improvements that many marketers ignore in favor of chasing the big solution, which will never come.

16

TRY A CAREER IN POLITICS

Earlier in the book I spoke of a complex, supposedly transformative project that went astray. Its ambitions were too vast, the moving pieces too many. Eventually the project owners found themselves pleading with the board for patience as they labored to reinvent the business. As you know, it didn't work.

I ran into one of the senior vice presidents who had sponsored the project one night at a joint along the cobblestone streets of the Meatpacking District in New York City. I could see from the glasses on the table that the group he was with had been there awhile. We had a good rapport and he was a few drinks in, which led to more honesty than you'd find at the average corporate soiree. I asked him how things were going.

He was almost too happy to answer.

"Look," he said. "I'm retiring. There's no upside in this project for me. I have to do it, because my boss wants to see it. I'll slog for the next couple of months across all of the steering committee meetings, board updates, and stand-ups, and I'll see absolutely nothing from it.

"If something goes wrong, I'll be on the receiving end of it. Maybe they'd even dock part of my bonus or stock. What's worse is whoever's replacing me is going to get all the credit once the project rolls out—'Oh, look, this new guy stepped in and then all of a sudden marketing performance went through the roof.'

"There's no reason for me to do this. I'm out."

To this day, I'm not sure if his participation would have been enough to see this transformation through. It was too bloated. Too many stakeholders. But it certainly wasn't going to happen without him.

It seems like I've just told you a business story, but this is actually a human story, a relationship story like all the others. Pitching a project based on data alone isn't going to seduce anybody. You need to understand— not assume—the motivations, emotions, and conditions that the others in the room bring to the table. Consider what's in their mind: *If I align myself with this person, or this idea, does it advance my prospects?*

That's not to say these people don't care. But they may have a different tolerance for risk because they have different incentives. We work with people who'll say, "You know what? I don't want to go after our high-value customers because these signals say that our offline program, which has eight hundred people sending out catalogs, is no longer efficient. I can't have that. I don't want to change it. I need my team and I need my budget." To be fair, this level of honesty would save us a lot of time. Oftentimes the same message comes across in a fifty-slide deck chock-full of data points on the revival of print.

Why You Need to Campaign

You can master the art of conversation and hold a deep interest in building long-term, rewarding customer relationships, but the success of these efforts is going to depend on the realities of your company. Egos, personalities and teams, winners and losers will restrict progress.

You will find differences between boards, executives, and employees. You'll find teams determined to protect their budgets and their fiefdoms. You'll find colleagues who are out to build empires and others who shrink from risk.

We can't talk about the promise of conversation and relationships without acknowledging how painful it can be to move organizations with measurement and data. We know that only 6 percent of marketing decisions are based on data.* About 50 percent are made based on personal experience, judgment, and intuition—a figure, interestingly enough, that doesn't vary whether you ask senior decision makers or junior decision makers. About 10 percent are made because of what the boss says, and another 10 percent because of what colleagues say.

How to Win Votes

It's not that people don't want to use data to make a decision. But there are lots of factors at play. If you find yourself in a situation in which people aren't moving or making changes, there are a few things you can do.

* Corporate Executive Board, "MREB Customer Focus Survey 2011."

READ THE ROOM

If you think it's sufficient to just put up a slide with the data that makes you passionate about a subject and expect your audience to respond with the same enthusiasm, you're fooling yourself. People love to talk up data-driven decisions because it sounds great, but the fact is that everyone interprets data through the lens of their role and their interests. What does your audience actually want to hear? If you're calling out a marketing program for bringing in poor customers, the team behind that program is going to challenge your case. You need to understand the incentives of the others in the room and whom they'll report back to afterward. If you don't think about your audience and how you're going to deliver your message in light of their interests, you'll encourage resistance, not progress.

GET CARDS ON THE TABLE

Different stakeholders will perceive the business in different ways, especially when it comes to customer expectations and the relationships that follow.

Our customers only care about price.

We need to recover our acquisition costs in six months.

We use this analytics platform as our source of truth.

It is valuable to explicitly identify these assumptions and their origin. (It's based on a test? Who ran the test? When? What methodology?) One of the common objections may come from someone who has explored customer lifetime value in the past. "We tried it." Or, more often, "I tried it when I worked at another company, and it failed." But using what methodology? How was it used? How was it measured?

DON'T MAKE PROMISES YOU CAN'T KEEP

You're entering an ambitious expanse with tremendous consequence, abandoning years of transactional behavior with customers for an approach that values them over a lifetime. As with any such project, it's counterproductive to simply declare, "We're going to use customer lifetime value from now on!" (You'd be surprised how many do.) Be more specific: "We're going to try calculating customer lifetime value, which requires these pieces of data, and we're going to compare the results in our reporting before taking any more action." There is nothing wrong with having a big vision. Taking smaller steps reduces anxiety about what's to come and allows the project to build on its own success.

AGREE TO HONOR THE RESULTS

Before you try something new, you need to get agreement from the affected teams on the actions you're going to take based on the results. All too often we work with companies that say, "We'll let the data decide."

The reality is that the most provocative and compelling programs stem from change within an organization. Change means doing something different. If we're investing in a new area, it's almost guaranteed that we're not investing in an old one. In order for there to be a perceived winner, there's likely to be a perceived loser.

When companies postpone a decision about how they'll act on an experiment's results until after it's completed, emotions come into play. People will tear apart the methodology and the insights a program produces based on how they feel about its findings and its implications for their role and their budget.

You need agreement up front. If it's at the executive level: Would we change our KPIs if we found out that acquiring better customers would be more profitable than just attracting any lead? Or within your marketing teams: If the test shows we should reallocate budgets, are we prepared to do it? Otherwise people will argue, and the results will never be used. The company goes into a state of paralysis. It's not pretty.

This isn't a comprehensive treatise on negotiation. I'm simply trying to call attention to the necessity of it. Decisions are not made based on data alone, ever, and you're not going to change the way people make decisions. They're going to consider not just your data but a variety of factors that include their own perspective, their role, their interests, and their own data, all of which will bias the outcome. You can't wish that away by saying, "Let's think of the company!" No one's going to rally around that flag.

But you can be aware of the rules of the game you're playing and the circumstances of the others who are playing it with you. As long as you understand the rules, you can navigate them. If you simply operate with blind optimism, trusting that the data will always win, you'll just run yourself into a wall.

17

UNLEASH
THE TESTERS

There were two advertisers. Both were in the travel industry, trying to reach the same customers. Minor differences aside, they were selling the same product. One afternoon, I gave them both the same research insight—a provocative little nugget about how consumers were making decisions for a particular international destination. The insight itself wasn't as fascinating as seeing how each company responded.

The CMO of the first company was appreciative, as always. "Well, that's fantastic!" he said. The requisite proclamation of "We're a data-driven company and we like to move quickly" followed, as did a test plan. It would take three to four weeks to build the experiment and gather the necessary approvals. Once everything was up and finished, he told me, we'd review the results together.

Then I called the leadership at the second company, who had the same amount of enthusiasm but followed it with this: "We'll have the test running by tomorrow."

Think about that. Both companies believed in experimentation and tested the idea. But one might get the results three weeks before its competitor—and this was just one test.

The first company ran three to four of these marketing tests a month. The second started forty to sixty tests each week. Which company's going to win? The one that gets more insights about its customers.

Why You Need to Learn Fast

Everything we've covered in this book is about understanding and communicating with your customers in a new and different way. But the fact is that trying new things is difficult for organizations. Existing priorities stand in the way. So does fear of risk, and the entrenched way we've always done things. It's counterintuitive for an organization that values success—both through praise and promotion—to pursue something that might not work. All that helps explain why the simple word *test* ramps up the ambitions of any marketer, but the potential for "failure" steers them toward hesitation.

You need new ideas. You need to test. You need to learn in order to survive and to grow, and you need to learn fast, because the best marketers and the best companies aren't waiting for you. So the question is, given all the obstacles, how do you unleash new ideas quickly? Not gathering everyone in a room for an afternoon of "brainstorming" but unlocking the possibilities from the data in front of you every day? How do you take a concept that makes others nervous and make it a little more comfortable, a little more palatable?

How to Make Testing a Habit

It's not necessarily enough to say, "Let's just run more tests." We once had a group visiting the campus that over lunch dropped the need to run more tests. When I asked what kind, they said, "We don't care, just give us any-thing. Even if it doesn't work." This led, unsurprisingly, to unnecessary spending, lost time, and few results. It turns out this company had decided to encourage more tests by tying everyone's bonuses to how often they ran them. Thirty tests per quarter was the magic number, and this group was behind.

That's not what we're going for.

Let's not talk about quotas. Let's talk about best practices—how to get better at testing.

UNCORK THE BOTTLE

The problem isn't having ideas for tests—it's bringing them to the surface. They're discovered by the people closest to the data, and they get lost on their way to the top. An analyst brings ten ideas to her boss, who says, "Hey, I can't pitch ten ideas to my CMO. Let's pick one." And that CMO is going to have five teams, and each gives him its top idea. Now he has five, but he can't fund five, so he picks the one that sounds like a sure thing. And all of the analysts shrug their shoulders and proclaim, "I wish my company were data driven."

Lots of great ideas get lost in these filters; there's not

the time or the money or the discipline to do them all. These bottlenecks slow the company down—and it's not because it doesn't have the opportunities.

GET EVERYONE IN

It's easy to get behind this: make testing a single, Marketing-wide process. Everyone sends their proposal to a single place. Use a spreadsheet or an online form. Just make sure you capture four things:

---

1. What's the hypothesis?

2. What data supports it?

3. How would you test it?

4. What would the company do differently, based on the results?

You're sidestepping all the bureaucracy. No silos. No filter. There are no titles, and there aren't even names. The form doesn't even ask where in the marketing department you sit. If the paid-search experts have an idea for social media, let them share it. The list is managed at the top, ideally by the CMO. We'll get to the part that they play in a moment.

This is an approach inspired by Google X.* It's actually how they run their "moonshot factory," charged with trying to solve the world's hardest problems.†

PUT UP A PRIZE

For most, the aspiration to run more tests can slam headfirst into the stagnant and stifling office culture: too many ideas that haven't made it anywhere, too many tests that aren't run often enough. You can try an email pep talk. You can try tying the number of tests to some performance review. But what works best in turning that stifling dynamic upside down is a contest. It's not just a new process but an opportunity. Put up a prize: cash, T-shirts, lunch with the boss. The goal is to motivate employees to start looking past legacy challenges and to start dreaming about what's possible with your

---

* For the record, Alphabet—formerly known as Google—rebranded Google X to just X.

† Peter H. Diamandis, "How to Run Wild Experiments Just Like (Google) X," Singularity Hub, April 28, 2016, https://singularityhub .com/2016/04/28/how-to-run-wild-experiments-just-like-google-x/.

data. A prize is a modest gesture that lets them know leadership is finally invested in it too.

REWARD IDEAS, NOT RESULTS

Here's the real secret to making this work: the prize is awarded before any tests are run. After all, the goal is not to recognize the sure thing, the safe bet. You probably don't even need to test those. The prize is for the best hypothesis that could leap the business forward. That's the whole point.

Now, at the end of the month, the executives are looking at a list of fifty to eighty to a hundred ideas, validated by their own data, put forth by their own team, a list of opportunities in front of the company that could be tested today. That shifts the thinking at the top. They see that they're sitting on millions of dollars in opportunities from their *existing* data and their *existing* people. Their sole purpose is to figure out how to get these tests done. Some companies have begun tracking the number of new ideas they generate and the number of tests they run in a spreadsheet, using the sum as a metric for innovation to guide their progress.

Suddenly the bottlenecks that stand in the way of testing new ideas come into focus too. Is it too difficult to figure out who is going to pay for it? Is the existing budget just too small for testing the volume of ideas you have? Is permission too difficult to come by? Updating the website or advertising too difficult?

Don't limit yourself to your own employees, either. Ask your partners, your ad networks, your agency to join in the contests. Every idea you get on the table is an opportunity to grow.

The process will make you progressively better—as it has the countless companies that have already embraced it.

Tips on Creating a Testing Culture

Everyone *wants* to take more risks and run more tests—but motivation alone is never enough. You can't simply will more experiments into existence.

ASK THE ANALYSTS

Most executives don't understand the reality of testing. If a CMO in love with their latest great idea says they want to run a test, I promise you it will get started with the utmost urgency. Everyone down the line will drop everything to make it happen.

But the more senior you are in an organization, the more limited your understanding of how difficult it is to test ideas in your company will be. Power and authority work wonders in getting things done, even if those things aren't the best use of the company's time, money, or talent.

The people with the best ideas are in there wrestling with your data on a daily basis, eager to make a difference if only they have the right opportunity. Just ask them. Understand the roadblocks they face in getting their insights put into action, or risk relegating them to dashboard duty.

IGNORE THE SILOS

CMOs are generally graded on specific metrics each quarter: revenue generated, sales made, or, quite often, the cost for each. When incentivized by these metrics, it's no surprise that they want to make sure every dollar goes toward driving them.

When things are going great, marketers tend to feel that they're dialed in, and they tend to just want to pour it on. "We're growing faster than we've ever grown. We're doing everything right. Why pull money from the sure thing? That's madness. It's our rocket fuel!"

Then the business flips. Marketing is behind its numbers. Every dollar counts in trying to close the gap. Keep things safe, simple, and defensible. Testing implies risk. It's not the time to try crazy new ideas—and so they don't.

The bottom line? It may seem like there is never a great time to test, despite your best intentions to one day, someday, get it going.

The best models I've seen start by pulling the experimentation budget separate from marketing—and its metrics—and tucking it under its own team. A few have even branded it Research & Development, a familiar term whose hint of future success makes it easier for CFOs to think of it as investment instead of spending. If nothing else, this shift gives the testers room to work instead of worrying about quarterly targets.

Just keep it simple: Did we learn something new about our customers? Yes or no.

KEEP IT REAL

This is one more thing that Amazon got right. Bezos broke down decisions into two categories.* Some can't be reversed. These are type 1 decisions. He insisted that they "be made methodically, carefully, slowly, with great deliberation and consultation." But most decisions can be changed; two-way doors, he called them. At Amazon, these type 2 decisions are made quickly, without rising to the top.

The bigger the organization, Bezos observed, the greater the tendency to apply type 1 rigor to type 2 decisions.

That's deadly, and the best companies avoid it. Some even do so with style. I worked with one company that named their tests based on the car they could have purchased with the money instead. They were always more careful to avoid crashing a Ferrari than a Camry.

* Jeff Haden, "Amazon Founder Jeff Bezos: This Is How Successful People Make Such Smart Decisions," Inc., December 3, 2018.

VISIT THE LIBRARY

Don't fall into the trap of thinking your challenges are so distinct that previous research is irrelevant, that every problem needs to be studied from scratch. There are areas of advertising where we've collected answers from thousands of tests. I can break down the results by vertical, by country, by company size, by time of day— and I'll still hear people say, "No, we need our own test because our situation is different." Is it, though?

There is a treasure trove of academic research at your fingertips. I've cited studies along the way that are available to anyone. They're published; they're out there. This research is more rigorous than what most companies could undertake on their own. Yet it's largely ignored because of that false sense of perceived uniqueness and—to be honest—because of the style in which it's written: forty pages of models and conclusions without a Power-Point slide in sight.

Bake it into your testing strategy: before you test, take a look and see what evidence might already be available.

DON'T PLAY TELEPHONE

You need to keep the distance between the people running the tests and the people making the decisions as short as possible. As the results work their way up the chain, it's common to see the findings slowly change to fit the narrative people want to tell.

It's rarely egregious. It's a game of telephone. Words get added; words get dropped. The nuance is lost. Take enough steps, and soon reality changes. Talk to the person who ran the experiment, not their manager and their manager's manager. You'll find the truth at the source.

BUILD INSIGHTS, NOT MONUMENTS

You've run a test, you've gained an understanding, and you're off and running! Well done! I don't want to bring you down, but as we've mentioned, nothing lasts forever. No matter how precious or provocative the insight, have an agreement as to when you're going to retest it. I've been part of projects where the origin of some assumptions—each holding serious weight in the decision to go forward—was unknown. In one company's case, I found that the churn rate of a customer base (*always* 3 percent each year, marketers alleged) had been established back in the nineties. Copied and pasted ever since.

*C*ompanies struggle not in generating new ideas but in putting them to work. Lots of stakeholders with a lot of competing interests could stand in the way. Establish a process of surfacing the ideas that are bubbling away in the hearts and minds of your team, and make it the mission of your leadership to test them. It's not enough to push through one idea or one change. Develop a culture of consistently raising ideas and putting them to the test. Some of your competitors are already testing dozens each week. They're not going to slow down for your benefit. You need to speed up.

18

BE FAITHFUL BUT NOT BLIND

The incoming sales director of a midsized B2B company was rightly concerned. Her predecessor had focused on incentivizing short-term, quota-hitting sales above all else. Customer satisfaction was low; churn was high. Buying a high-value contract one month might not even merit a follow-up call until you were ready to commit to a second.

The new director was hired for exactly that reason. She knew that what you incentivize you get. She wanted her sales teams to emphasize partnership and strategic growth, to think of themselves as business Yodas, not just sellers. To encourage the changes, she set a basic metric: an engagement quota.

Sales teams would be measured not just by revenue but by the number of meaningful conversations they had with their clients. Each conversation was a point on their customer-engagement scoreboard. Meet your revenue and your engagement quotas, get a larger bonus; fall short, and get a little less.

New metrics, new dashboards, a new accountability. Operations reported a 300 percent boost in client engagements. The salespeople got bigger bonuses. The ops team, praised for its process-driven savvy, got promotions.

Only customer behavior didn't change. A follow-up test treated one set of customers the same as they always had while giving another set more attention. Both spent the same amount of money. The company's conclusion: their industry thrived on transactional relationships— deeper connections didn't matter.

Or they just screwed the whole thing up. You decide.

The sales director wanted to measure customer engagement but was worried about harming the autonomy of the sales teams. She didn't want to be too prescriptive. She didn't want to say only sixty-minute phone conversations with SVPs or above, because that's not how business works. So she set a more open quota that became subject to interpretation by the sales teams. I spoke to some of them about it.

"So does a phone call with the executives count?"

"Absolutely."

"What about an email?"

"Definitely. We cover the same stuff as a phone call, sometimes more."

"What if they email you back?"

"That'd be a second engagement."

The engagement metric failed, bringing the strategy down with it, because everyone accepted the numbers for what they were. As soon as Ops started getting praise and promotions, they were out. Did salespeople really want to return their bonuses?

The result was a senior leader who saw great numbers that told an empty story.

Metrics matter—and good metrics can make all the difference in helping you identify your best customers and find more like them. We've covered that. But here's another simple truth: any metric can be manipulated with the right incentive. And it will be.

I once led a workshop exercise with a company that was part publisher, part retailer. We broke the team into small groups, assigning each one a KPI from their existing dashboards. For six rounds, each team competed to present an approach for improving their metric. To the victors we offered a serious prize: an extra day off—enough of an incentive to wake them up from a day that was otherwise filled with endless vision statements and stock photography.

The first round was vanilla corporate, with teams offering up various translations of their existing plans. Bullet-pointed plans for improvement.

"We're going to grow ad-impression volume by providing superior thought leadership and insights to our users."

By the third or fourth round, things became interesting. Teams started to push.

"We're going to grow ad-impression volume 2x by doubling the number of ad placements that we have on each page."

Other teams grumbled, especially those that recognized the consequences. Lower click-through rates. Diluted value for advertisers. But that's not the metric we were judging the team by. Their metric was ad impressions. And that really set things off.

A different team:

"We'd split the shipping and billing information to two different pages. Oh! And if we deprecate our store's search engine, people will probably need to click on more pages to find the products they are looking for."

There was the engineer who went for the throat:

"We're going to reduce our server capacity so pages take longer to load. I don't really care, because time on-site for anyone left will go up."

And the outsourcing expert:

"Let's just buy half a million social media followers from Eastern Europe. It should only cost a few hundred dollars, making it the highest-ROI campaign we've ever run."

Nothing incurred the collective wrath more than this one. I tried to mediate: *How are you evaluating the quality of the social media traffic you get today?*

They weren't. Nobody was.

Why You Need to Get Inside Your Metrics

The point of the workshop isn't that you need bulletproof metrics. The point is that you need to consider carefully how your metrics could be influenced—purposefully or not. You need to understand the levers that can be pulled for a metric and the consequences of doing so. If you don't, you're in trouble. Bulletproof ones are nearly impossible to come by. Revenue may be cash in the bank, but I can give you a list of companies that use cheap gimmicks to front-load that figure right as their stock is about to vest. While you may not have a leader who egregiously adds new advertising placements to your site or buys cheap followers, you may have teams that split placements as part of a UI redesign, or a social media team that doesn't vet the quality of the traffic a partner delivers.

One mistake a lot of companies make in incentivizing misbehaviors is pushing only on their underperforming metrics. If you go into the boardroom with green numbers, you'll receive praise more than scrutiny. Go in with red numbers and get ready to play defense.

The best companies look at great numbers and underperforming numbers with the same rigor. That means if you have great numbers and can't explain what you did in a way that's repeatable, or you have an overperforming sector and can't tell your less fortunate colleagues what strategies you embraced, you're not going to get recognized for great numbers at all. The message is explicit. The methods matter as much as the metrics, and leaders won't accept the metrics if they aren't understandable or repeatable.

How to Keep Your Numbers from Lying

There are many ways to approach the challenge of getting inside your metrics and what they mean. One to consider is "red teaming," a concept borrowed from the CIA.*

When the CIA reviews an analysis, they'll assign a small group of people with no skin in the game to find its weaknesses. That's their goal. It's a mission they can't decline. Same data, same research question—and their job is to make the best case for a different answer. Most analysts will write their paper in hopes of leading the director to the decision they want him to make. The red team gives them a different point of view.

Leading companies have adapted this approach to

---

* Micah Zenko, "Inside the CIA Red Cell," *Foreign Policy*, October 30, 2015.

their own cultures. Instead of relying entirely on a product owner who may have incentives to guide a particular decision in their favor—or may not be able to see beyond their own silo—they'll assign a cross-functional team of several analysts to write their own counterpositions to substantive programs before the top executives make their call. What's missing? Where could things go wrong?

These teams report directly to the executive team and are rotated every few months to prevent their own agendas from taking hold.

If you can't build a team, find an outside adviser who can provide the same level of candor. Their goal isn't to tell you what to do. It's not to make the decision for you. It's to make sure that you can consider an independent viewpoint before making a decision, lest you risk a surge of social media followers from Moldova.

Once you put a process like this in place, you'll realize a second benefit that's kind of fun: project owners start to become more transparent. If you know a team is going to write a counterposition to your idea, you want to get in front of that—because otherwise you'll look like you either skipped something on purpose or weren't smart enough to realize it in the first place.

See the Other Side

A group of researchers gave twenty-nine teams the same data and the same question: Are soccer referees more likely to give red cards to dark-skinned players than to light-skinned players? In findings published by the Association for Psychological Science, they reported that the twenty-nine teams took twenty-one different analytical approaches.* Twenty said yes, there was statistically significant evidence of bias; nine disagreed.

"These findings suggest that significant variation in the results of analyses of complex data may be difficult to avoid, even by experts with honest intentions," the researchers wrote. They concluded that it may be advantageous to have different researchers study the same problem, because it helps to highlight the subjective analytical choices that influence the results and thus the decisions you base on them.

* R. Silberzahn et al., "Many Analysts, One Data Set: Making Transparent How Variations in Analytic Choices Affect Results," *Advances in Methods and Practices in Psychological Science* 1, no. 3 (September 2018): 337–56.

*U*sing data successfully involves more than painting by numbers. It requires an understanding of how the metrics are calculated—and how they can be driven in ways both meaningful and manipulative. If you're not acting on this knowledge, you may be getting played. Surround yourself with processes, silly or serious, to get that knowledge on the table. The result will be greater transparency and better performance.

19

FIELD A WINNING TEAM

S ome people can make a project successful. Others will torch every project they touch. It helps if you can tell them apart.

Let's start with the practitioners of the dark corporate arts. Avoid those people if you can—but you really can't, so you need to learn how to manage them. The first step in that direction is recognizing them for what they are.

The Uninspired Detractors

THE EFFICIENCY EXPERTS

Efficiency experts have two rallying cries. The first is "I want to know where to put my next dollar." Right? They always use one dollar, which is bizarre. I suppose it means they want to be that granular. They insist on strict accountability as a prerequisite for getting anything done.

The second is the quote widely attributed to John Wanamaker: "Half the money I spend on advertising is wasted; the trouble is I don't know which half."* If the efficiency expert is giving a presentation, this is *always* the second slide in the deck. Efficiency experts want the

---

* The quote is widely attributed to Wanamaker within a number of texts, including David Ogilvy's popular 1963 book *Confessions of an Advertising Man* (pp. 86–87). That said, a number of researchers have struggled to find evidence of Wanamaker ever making that statement, with some arguing that it was actually made by Lord Leverhulme. Again, evidence there is scant. But it is a terrific quote, and someone must have been the first to say it!

answer—or at least enjoy putting others through the chase.

Self-righteous curmudgeons. They slow any marketing organization, because they lock in on the question of accountability: measuring the precise return of marketing investment.

It may seem pretty positive. Who can argue with accountability? But when you spend so much time trying to figure out where that mythical dollar goes, you raise the bar for the new opportunities you could invest in. Experimenting with new ideas can be a terribly inefficient process, at least at first, because you have much to learn. So rather than waste that dollar, the efficiency experts don't spend it.

This is where companies stagnate. At a certain point, their budgets get so large that efficiency is the only question they dwell on. They stop investing in risky things, they place only safe bets, avoid new tactics—and they don't go anywhere.

You want efficiency, but not efficiency experts. Let them run supply chains or call centers. And make sure 10 percent of your marketing budget is always tucked aside for exploration. Put it outside the efficiency scope. Measure the results not by the dollars that come back but by what you learn. It's the key to driving your business forward.

THE PERFECTIONISTS

These are the research-oriented types who treat every project as a corporate dissertation. They want to make big contributions and rely on uncompromising models, immaculate experiments, and journal accolades as their measure of success. The challenge in their brilliance is that most businesses struggle to create the environment they need to thrive. They're obsessed with the perfect answer, and the messy world of digital measurement is anything but perfect.

You want these people on your team because they will challenge others. They will raise the bar, bringing a certain amount of discipline and rigor to measurement— one that's often missing on teams built entirely of practitioners. The problem is there's a practical reality about the amount of risk you need to accept for a business to move forward. Without the proper structure, perfectionists become a roadblock. Perfectionists would take years to study problems when the market is moving in weeks.

If you hire these people, you need to be purposeful about the work you assign them and the message you send in doing it. Stress the opportunity cost of studying a problem to perfection. Emphasize the reversibility of decisions. Make clear that accepting risk is intentional and inescapable. Find projects where their attention to detail is required—the big budgets and other business decisions that aren't easily reversed—but frame even these with the reality that the larger organization needs to move quickly to survive. Most important, share the rationale behind your thinking. Imperfect decisions driven by a business imperative to act are acceptable to this group. Haphazard choices to satisfy arbitrary deadlines or egos are not.

THE INSECURE

A lot of what I've talked about is using data to predict customer relationships—looking into the future and asking questions. Is this particular relationship worth my time? Is this person going to stick around and spend a lot of money with us? Is that person going to leave?

None of those predictions mean anything if you're desperately trying to retain customers at all costs. The insecure will spend highly to attract high-value customers, which makes sense . . . and then they'll keep investing in them, for fear they will go someplace else. That doesn't make sense. The reason they're high value is that the model predicts they're going to stay. Spending more on them only degrades their value. It's just lost money.

When the model says a relationship has low value, they'll say, "We've got to increase our spend." When the model says a relationship has run its course, the insecure won't let go. They've got to win that customer back.

Left unchecked, they'll give away the profits you would have captured and blame techniques such as customer lifetime value for being the wrong strategy.

The only way to manage the insecure is experimentation. Divide a pool of customers in two. Leave one be and let the insecure intervene with the other. Did those customers really spend more? Did they really stick around longer? Was any of it worth the hassle?

The insecure can be saved, but they have to see the light. They have to witness it firsthand and see the test results.

The Difference Makers

THE STORYTELLERS

Theirs is a rare talent. Seek them out. Develop them. Cherish them.

These are the people who have fluency and enough respect for the models to be credible guides to the analysts, while also understanding how to translate the opportunity to others in the organization. Storytellers know how to engage their colleagues in Finance, Sales, Marketing, or Product Development on their own terms, helping them see the opportunities within the context of their own experiences and mindset. They shape opinions and build enthusiasm; the best of them create new evangelists to carry the message forward.

Too many teams don't recognize the need for storytelling, so they don't hire for it. They hire more people like themselves, with hard math skills. Nothing wrong with that—if they're working on cloud infrastructure. But number crunchers aren't the right people to convince a sales team to care.

You need people who can build bridges, who can explain the long-term value model you're building to the

CFO, who can talk with Operations about what they need to build to reach high-value customers. You need people who can tell the story that makes your insight so convincing that it's almost intuitive to the person on the other end.

THE ENTREPRENEURS

There are many moving pieces inside organizations, and progress can be stopped in its tracks by an obstacle as simple as getting everyone to show up to a meeting, never mind bringing them into agreement on a new direction. While focusing on short, actionable wins and building a collection of storytellers will help, teams benefit when they include a specific type of generalist—the entrepreneur—to help move them forward. Not the one who has written a business plan or raised a round of funding but the one who has worked in small teams to set up infrastructure and deploy marketing, make landing pages and run tests, all under tight deadlines with little support. Nothing they build will approach the caliber larger organizations expect, but that's not the point. They serve as a catalyst. Living enzymes. They get things moving by adding new, dynamic capabilities to a team that's just trying to get something done.

THE STUDENTS

We stand on the shoulders of giants: a field of customer analytics built from the research and brilliance of academic heavyweights including Peter Fader, Bruce Hardie, and Daniel McCarthy. It stands to reason that the next generation of innovation will come, in turn, from their students. A generation that can bake those lifetime-value cakes and also understand the ingredients, the methods, and how to stretch them into new applications.

Not only can you hire those students—especially those in Professor Fader's infamous MKTG 476 course at Wharton—but these professors also make many of their lectures available online through a variety of platforms.

Either seek these students out or commit yourself to the coursework and become one yourself.*

* I keep a running list of lectures and courses on my website.

If you're not living in a superhero movie, you need to learn to identify the attributes of actual human beings who make your team better. And you need to identify the attributes of those who don't play well with others, even if their behavior isn't detrimental on its own, and adjust for it. Resist the temptation to solve a problem by adding a bunch of new members to your team. Bringing on one better person or pushing out a single wrong person can have a huge impact. Nobody said building a great team was easy. In fact, it's hard work, but it needs to be done.

CONCLUSION

I hope you're intoxicated by what you've read. We began our journey by talking about conversations and how to engage others in ways that build genuine understanding of their needs. We talked about relationships and how to identify the people who matter. We talked about self-improvement and how to build a culture that fosters exploration and taking risks. My goal in sharing what I've learned was to inspire more questions than I answered, because that's the next step in the journey—only now we're on it together.

The first time that I presented these lessons to a client, I went in hard. I began with the breakdown of their customers, from the most valuable to the least. First slide. You remember what that looks like from earlier. Same thing.

Customer Segment	Average Value / Person	Total Value	% of Revenue
1	$3,200	$283,200,000	81%
2	$350	$30,975,000	9%
3	$200	$17,700,000	5%
4	$120	$10,620,000	3%
5	$80	$7,080,000	2%

Figure 8.4

I described the methodology and the peer-reviewed research behind the calculations. Here are the attributes of your high-value customers, I explained, as well as the people you should target and the people you should avoid. Here's how to move your money—and how much you'll make when you do. The same lessons we explored in this book I enthusiastically compressed into a breathless twenty-minute presentation for my clients.

So clear. So convincing. I paused for agreement.

"So . . . ," the chairman said. "You built a model that says that we should invest more money in our customers today, then wait months to see how those relationships pay off? We won't let Marketing or anyone else spend without accountability. We spend today. Customers buy today or they don't. That's it."

Well, that was a curveball. And my numbers were so good!

I learned something important that day: it's better to help others find their own questions than it is to just hand them answers. Curiosity and wonder will carry an organization further than blind faith, no matter how convincing the evidence.

Today, I begin with the very same slide and a much shorter narrative: "Here is how your customers are predicted to spend with you. As of today, we're spending and messaging to each of them in the same way."

And then I stop and take questions. And the attendees let them fly.

"Well, how confident are you in these numbers?"

"What can we do to bring in more of the top customers?"

"Who is responsible for bringing in all of the terrible ones?"

"Why shouldn't we be spending more on those that are buying the most from us?"

So it goes. The people in the room lead themselves along the same journey that this book has taken you on. They build their own understanding and intuition. Only then can they contribute their own ideas, join in the process, and support the transformation a business needs to make this approach successful.

I don't want you to put down this book, build a deck, and shout, "Here's the direction we need to go!" I want you to teach, to listen, to let others be curious about customer relationships and contribute their own ideas for consideration. To help others in your business—in your field—grow with you.

This is how you become a legend. Not only because of the results you deliver but by the following you build and the vision you allow others to share in.

People—your customers, your colleagues, your investors—will be grateful to be in your company.

See you out there,

—Neil

Why don't we continue this conversation online? I built
a small website for you to ask questions, meet others,
and find tools that will help you on your journey.

http://convertedbook.com

ACKNOWLEDGMENTS

I'd like to thank Mark Travis, who as a true literary craftsman inspired, encouraged, and questioned my thinking throughout the writing process. Absent his provocations, this book may have found itself resembling a corporate memorandum—without structure, voice, or conviction, and likely unread.

To the editors, copywriters, marketers, and publicists at Penguin Random House, appreciation for their committed efforts in bringing these ideas to the world. I'm especially grateful for Noah Schwartzberg, Kimberly Meilun, and Margot Stamas, who served as indispensable guides as I crossed into the publishing world for the first time.

To my literary agent, Jim Levine, thank you for sharing a lifetime of experience and advice exactly when I needed it. Particular gratitude is due to the team at Fortier Public Relations. Led by Mark Fortier and Maria Mann, they were relentless in bringing this book and its ideas to new corners of the world.

My research in this field of marketing would be empty if not for the research and mentorship of Peter Fader. Few can match his contributions to the field of customer analytics, and none can come close to the generosity he offers to those who are pursuing the same.

To my colleagues at Google who I've had the privilege of working alongside over the past decade: I'm incredibly proud of the work that we've accomplished together, but perhaps even more grateful for the advice, challenges, and mentorship that you've shared at pivotal points in my career. To Alan Moss, Alex Chinien, Allan Thygesen, April Anderson, Avinash Kaushik, Charlie Vestner, Jane Hong, Jim Lecinski, John McAteer, Rachel Zibelman, Ted Souder, Tom Bartley, and countless others: thank you!

Of course, none of this would have been possible without Alan Eagle, Nicolas Darveau-Garneau, and the wider Google evangelist team. Supporters who gave me the confidence to pursue this project in the first place. A thoughtful sounding board for ideas, an unending stream of encouragement, and a group that I am truly blessed to work alongside each day.

My appreciation extends across a small but extraordinary group of friends, including Chris von Burske, David Cooley, Frank Cespedes, Kevin Buerger, Mark Dannenberg, Michael Loban, Raghu Iyengar, Tony Kam, and Sarah Norman, who each shaped this book in their own unique and invaluable way.

And, finally, to my family: I exist because of your love, patience, and sacrifice. I hope that this particular adventure has made you proud.

INDEX

Note: Page numbers in *italics* refer to figures or tables.